PLANNING, PREPARING, PRAISING

PLANNING, PREPARING, PRAISING

Worship Resources for the Laity

Murray J. S. Ford
Emrys M. Jenkins

JUDSON PRESS ® VALLEY FORGE

PLANNING, PREPARING, PRAISING

Copyright © 1978
Judson Press, Valley Forge, PA 19481

Unless otherwise indicated, Bible quotations in this volume are in accordance with the Revised Standard Version of the Bible, copyrighted 1946, 1952, 1971, 1973 © by the Division of Christian Education of the National Council of the Churches of Christ in the United States of America, and are used by permission.

Other versions of the Bible quoted in this book are:

The Holy Bible, King James Version.

The New English Bible, Copyright © The Delegates of the Oxford University Press and The Syndics of the Cambridge University Press, 1961, 1970.

The Jerusalem Bible, Copyright © Doubleday & Company, Inc., 1966.

Library of Congress Cataloging in Publication Data

Ford, Murray J. S.
  Planning, preparing, praising.

  Bibliography: p. 93.
  1. Public worship. 2. Worship programs. I. Title.
BV25.F56   264   78-3475
ISBN 0-8170-0798-9

The name JUDSON PRESS is registered as a trademark in the U.S. Patent Office. Printed in the U.S.A.

Dedicated to those persons, in many churches, whose interest in the lay leadership of worship has inspired us to complete this book.

CONTENTS

Introduction   9

1   **Worship in Small Group Meetings**   11

2   **Sanctuary Worship**   27

3   **Resources for Advent**   49

4   **Resources for Lent**   57

5   **Personal and Interpersonal Worship**   67

6   **Sources of Ideas for Worship**   77

7   **Aids to Worship**   89

Resources   93

Index   95

INTRODUCTION

Christian liturgy in all areas of the church has gone through tremendous change. The Roman Catholic's Vatican II led to the dropping of Latin and a turn to the vernacular and to an infusion of new music and new worship forms. The free or reform tradition changed, but not as dramatically. Even though in many ways we still are complacent about our worship, we are beginning to expand our ideas to include new ways to worship.

Worship has been understood as a minister or priest standing before the people leading them in worship. In the new movement of worship, the people have become less passive and more active in worship; they have words to say and things to do. The minister or priest is no longer the only "leader" in worship; he or she is more the "chairperson" of worship. Consequently, the lay person becomes one of the leaders instead of just a responder.

More and more Christians find themselves in positions of leading worship experiences. Some of these acts seem very simple—reading the Scriptures from the Bible on the pulpit or lectern, for example. When it comes to prayers, orders of worship, appropriate things to say in a devotion, it is not always so easy. Often they turn to their ministers and ask, "Do you have a book that will help me with this prayer?" Very often the minister has a handbook or two that offer some resources, but they seem *ministerial* and are not quite what lay persons have in mind.

To help meet the need within the church, we, the authors, felt a handbook for the occasions on which lay persons find themselves leaders in worship is a growing necessity. Though we do not claim that this is either the best or the only resource, we do hope that it will be a helpful one both to lay persons asked to lead in worship and to ministers or priests in helping them to see the potential for lay leadership.

While some of the resources included—for example, prayers to be used before the distribution of the bread and wine at Communion— have traditionally been linked with certain denominations, we feel that they can also have value for other traditions.

We have outlined a number of possible formats that are usable in a variety of situations, but it is our hope that the main thrust of this handbook will be to show the reader how to prepare his or her own worship style. Worship is a very personal matter, and how you lead worship should mirror your own vocabulary and not merely reflect that of others.

1

WORSHIP IN SMALL GROUP MEETINGS

Many times people find themselves involved in conducting worship in the context of a meeting which is not primarily a service of worship. Sometimes this is referred to as "taking devotions." We would stress that worship in this kind of situation should be not too long, not too short!

The length of the worship act in a general meeting can be a problem. If the act is superficial, abrupt, offhanded, it may not be appropriate at all. In fact, it should not be considered worship. On the other hand, there is a tendency by some people to see worship as what is done in the sanctuary by the clergy. Thus, they decree that we have not worshiped unless all the elements of "sanctuary worship" have been included.

We need to separate our understanding of the word "worship" from what happens in the sanctuary and discover that it means showing devotion and reverence to God. All exercises of worship ought to do this. If we accept this concept, we can understand the intent of worship—any act of worship. The word "reverence" means to have a feeling of deep respect, love, and awe. Devotion means to show affection. Thus, worship is not a ritual or a means of teaching; it is, rather, an expression of our loyalty and faithfulness to God. It is an expression and confirmation of our love for God. It is a reconfirmation of our covenant with our God.

If this sense of worship is maintained, it does not matter where in the general meeting it takes place. It may change the actual content, but it will not change the attitude and feeling of the act of worship.

When asked to lead such a devotion, you need to know in what part of the meeting it will take place. You need to know what will come before and what will come after the worship. You need to know the intent of the meeting and the general topic of the guest speaker or major presentation. You then need to decide whether you will relate to any of these influences—and if so, how—or thus fulfill an expression of veneration of God.

One rule which must be recognized is that the purpose for which the group meets must occupy the major portion of the meeting and the devotion is not intended to replace it or to dominate it.

It may be difficult for the devout worshiper to accept the fact that the worship should be a secondary aspect of the meeting. When you look at your life, however, you will recognize that a relatively minor part of your life is spent in the overt expression of devotion—that is, in prayer, meditation, and responding to Scripture. The major portion of any meeting is an expression of our interests, concerns, and knowledge requirements. Our involvement sprouted because of our God-concern. The devotional is an outward expression of an inward attitude that prevails in our lives and more specifically, for that moment, in the meeting.

As shortness may denote superficiality, so long-windedness can mean a lack of understanding of the intent of worship. It can also show disrespect for those who have been asked to prepare the major portion of the meeting's agenda. As a general rule, something that is over ten minutes or under two minutes is either too long or too short.

If our assumption that many persons cannot separate their concept of worship from all the elements included in "sanctuary worship" is right, the major danger in conducting a small group devotion is to be overly long. Therefore, the primary need in leading worship in a small group is to have the proper attitude, and the thing to guard against is getting too involved and lengthy. Having determined that the time should be somewhere between two and ten minutes and that our attitude in worship ought to declare our devotion and respect to God, we can now look at forms and content without seeing them as just liturgical formulas.

Variety in worship is necessary only if it is going to last twenty minutes or more; so within the time frame set for devotions only two, or at the most three, changes of pace are necessary. Since prayer is the most natural expression of devotion, it must be a dominant part of the devotions. Opening sentences, Scriptures, hymns, and readings are other options. All of these are available from various sources, but the prayer tends to be a personal expression. Though there are prayers that are readable and can be made to fit the occasion, be true to your own expression.

When you use your own prayers, you can either pray spontaneously using your own words or write out the prayer in advance. The problem with extemporaneous prayer is the inconsistent quality of wording and of thought. Unless you are a fluent thinker on your feet, this is not the best way. Even when the words seem to flow, you will find that you are using phrases that recur quite often, such as "We just pray, Lord," or "We just thank you, Lord," etc. If you write the prayer more often than you extemporize, you will avoid repetition of these pat phrases; your impromptu prayers will improve.

Whenever you are leading in worship, remember always that you are within the community. You are not being judged by others who are better than you in the sight of God. You are God's child, and what you bring in love is accepted. If you offer praise and commitment even in the shakiest of voices, it is acceptable to him. The question is not how God will receive it, but whether you feel it worth expressing well. If you wish to offer your best to God in a meaningful way, then the onus is on you to work to present what is your own best. Having said that, some of your work could be finding what is the best of others which will express what you feel needs to be said. What we are suggesting is that your humility may demand that you seek others who are "better," but the danger is to make the leading of devotions so removed from you that the devotional character is lost. The ideal is for worship to be real and personal. If it is neither, it becomes a simple exercise in selection.

The following are some examples of written prayers that we feel are usable in your small group worship. We invite you to use them. We would also like to make some observations about them. You can use these observations with the prayers as your worship, or you can use them as guidelines in developing your own worship. We do not feel that these guidelines are absolutes but, rather, just starters for learning how to pray and stimulating your own confidence.

General Meditations for Small Group Meetings

Wonder (Psalm 8:4-6)

In the middle of this beautiful psalm which speaks of the glory and majesty of God are three verses that speak more directly of humankind. When compared to the moon and the stars, humankind seems like such a minute part of the total creation. And yet, God has made us only a little lower than himself and has given us dominion over the works of God's hands.

It is difficult to reflect on the tremendous heritage given over to us without wondering just how far this has extended. As we worry about the proliferation of atomic power and the disposal of atomic wastes, we wonder just how far our power has extended.

How important, then, that we return to the reaffirmation found in verses 1-3 and 7-9! The majesty, the power, the love, and the goodness of God are there in bold relief, and it is these that will keep everything in perspective.

May our brief reflection on these verses lead us to a deeper commitment to our Creator God and to the role he has allowed us to play in his world. May we never seek to usurp his place and think of ourselves more highly than we ought to think.

PRAYER:

O Lord, our Lord, how majestic is your name! We acknowledge your creation and preservation in all of our lives. We take into frail and trembling hands the tasks you have given to us. Never leave us to our own resources or allow us to think of ourselves more highly than we ought to think. In our wonder may we praise and serve you in humble gratitude for all your love to us.

In Jesus' name we pray.   Amen.

Life in Christ (2 Corinthians 4:14-16)

The Apostle has encountered several factors in the Corinthian church that need correction. After he deals with these problems in his letter to the Corinthian church, he moves on to assert confidence in his ministry and apostleship. Despite all of the persecution and opposition (7-15), he is not downcast or discouraged; the life he proclaims in Christ will triumph over the death that is at work in the world.

And now, in these two verses he comes to a magnificent summation of it all. The life in Christ, as he has been raised from the dead, will regenerate us, and this grace will extend to more and more people. The Apostle invites us to join him in the sure and certain knowledge that God has acted decisively in Christ and will continue to save all who will respond.

(Read verses 14-16.)

Verse 16 says, "So we do not lose heart." What a confident affirmation for the people of God! If the Apostle in the midst of all his troubles could be so confident, how can we allow our little trials to overcome us?

PRAYER:

O God, forgive us for our failure of nerve, our tendencies to think that our efforts are more important than our dependency upon you. As we hear the words of the Scripture, may they speak to our deepest need. May the life in Christ become our possession so that we will never lose heart.

In the name of the One who overcame death for us, we pray.

Amen.

Be Strong in the Lord (Ephesians 6:10-20)

The final chapter of the book of Ephesians depicts the real purpose of the Christian's commitment. Christians are urged to put on the whole armor of God in order to defend themselves against their enemies. They are not expected to depend upon themselves or their own resources. Indeed, the enemies are far too powerful and subtle for that. Christians are to don all of the available protection and go forth in the knowledge that they are never alone.

(Read verses 10-20 of Ephesians 6.)

We are not contending against flesh and blood, but against principalities and powers. There are probably no more contemporary words than these in all of the New Testament. They really have direct application to the twentieth century, especially as we have been tempted to depend upon our own strengths (military or other forms of coercion) rather than God's. Be strong in the Lord and in his power. It is only there that true strength can be found.

PRAYER:

O God, we beg your forgiveness for all of the times we have succumbed to the temptation to depend upon our own power. Help us to be open, much more open than ever before, to the tremendous resources you have made available to us in Jesus Christ. May the release of your power extend to all persons and bring your peace to the world.

In his name and for his sake, we pray.   Amen.

The People Are Too Many (Judges 6–7)

The constantly recurring theme heard in recent years is that the church is losing members; it just isn't going to be able to carry on. A most interesting story is told in the book of Judges about Gideon, whom the Lord had chosen to lead the army of Israel. The enemy at the time were the Midianites. The people of Israel were prone to attribute all of their successes both in war and peace to their own unaided strength, and God wanted there to be no possibility this time that they would think they had won any battles without his help.

So Gideon, in that familiar story, first sent home those who admitted to being afraid. Of thirty-two thousand, ten thousand were left. Next he took them to the water, and everyone who got down and lapped water for a drink was sent home; only those who scooped the water up in their hands were retained. Gideon was left with three hundred men. Their strategy was to attack the Midianite camp at night, blow trumpets, smash jars, and light torches. The resulting panic caused the enemy to flee in disarray, and Gideon's few men had the victory given to them.

This is a beautiful and simple story much needed in the twentieth century. We often are tempted to place too much importance on numbers and financial strength and forget that our strength is in the Lord. It is too easy to think of our denomination, or our church, or our group as ours, as our personal possession to do with as we please. Not so, these are God's; and to the extent they do his will, they will be blessed. When they cease to do so, they need correction.

PRAYER:

We have, our Father, thought of ourselves more highly than we ought to think. We have failed to give you credit for your goodness in our lives. Like Gideon of old, we stop and reflect.

Take our minds off things material and numerical. Help us to do only your will and be only your people, even at the cost of being out of step with the world.

In the name of Christ we pray.   Amen.

"In Him Was Life. . . ." (John 1:1-5)

It is a good thing to be reminded of our rootage in creation. Both

Genesis and John begin by taking us back to the beginning in the mind and heart of God the Creator. "All things were made by him; and without him was not any thing made that was made" (John 1:3, KJV). The real message, however, is that "in him was life . . ." (John 1:4a, KJV). It has been the purpose of God from the beginning that we live in the life he gives, and that life is seen most clearly in Christ. (Read John 1:1-5.)

On one occasion I heard the great E. Stanley Jones speak to a small group on a blizzardy night in Brooklyn, New York. He talked of the life and mission of the people of God and of their constant responsibility to be in mission. He summed it up in these unforgettable words: "The church that ceases to bleed is the church that ceases to bless." The light has been let loose in our midst, and we are called to respond to that light and live our lives by that light. Our mission is to spread the light and dissipate the darkness.

PRAYER:

Shine once more, O God, into our darkened lives. Help us to throw open the shutters that your light may come in and illumine and cleanse. May we not turn our backs to the light and life you give, and may it be that we shall be a company of those who share the life with all whom we meet day by day.

In Christ's name we pray.   Amen.

"You Are Witnesses" (Luke 24:44-49)

Some years ago James Reston, the renowned editorial writer of the *New York Times,* wrote about our times: "They are the best of times, the worst of times." Put this together with the phrase from the last chapter of Luke, "You are witnesses of these things" (v. 48), and you have a provocative pair of utterances. What can they say to us today?

We are doubtless living in a time of great contrasts. Never have we seen such destruction and despair; yet never have the exploits of speed and space been so impressive.

(Read Luke 24:44-49.)

If we are to cope with the extreme "ups and downs" of our civilization, we need the rootage of which these verses speak. We are witnesses to the fact that God continues to act. These few verses are a neat summary of the heart of the gospel. God loves; he sent his Son, his only Son, to live and die for the world; he raised him from the dead and offers forgiveness and salvation to all persons. Of all of this we are witnesses, and it is our responsibility to give the most accurate and compelling account possible. We need to think of ourselves as a "witnessing community"—anything less is inadequate.

PRAYER:

O God, you have acted out your love on the world's stage, and we have been witnesses. May we go out each day in the sure and certain knowledge that we do have a story to tell, a story of faith and love which needs to be told until all have heard.

In the name of our blessed Lord we pray.   Amen.

Be Still (Psalm 40:1-8)

"Be still, and know that I am God. I am exalted among the nations" (Psalm 46:10). What a strange contrast such an idea brings to our modern, noisy world! All around us are record players, radios, tapes, TVs, intercoms—all sending one or another form of noise into our ears.

Jesus frequently took the disciples aside from the press of the crowds to a quiet place for reflection. There they prayed to God, and Jesus taught them the lessons of eternal truth they needed to learn. It is not always easy for us to go apart from our busy living patterns, but we ought to take as many opportunities as we can to compose ourselves before God.

Psalm 40 expresses something of the same fervent hope. The psalmist waits patiently for the deliverance of God. He is bogged down with the woes of life; and except God delivers, there is little hope for him.

(Read Psalm 40:1-8).

Let us calm our desires to be hyperactive, constantly to be at the center of the noise and the furor. Let us retreat to a quiet place and let the healing restorative powers of the Almighty flow into our hearts.

PRAYER:

We would be still, O God, that we may know we need your presence, your power, and your great love in our lives. Teach us to trust, to depend upon you both now and always.

In the name of our great example we pray.   Amen.

Meditations for Church Business Meetings

All Together in One Place (Acts 2:1-4)

One of the most attractive stories of the young church as depicted in the Acts of the Apostles is found in chapter 2. Verse 1 states quite simply: "They were all together in one place." A lot of clergy and church leaders would give plenty to see such an event duplicated. Someone has quipped that this was probably the first and the last such demonstration of total unanimity. Seriously, though, there is a profound teaching embodied in these words.

(Read Acts 2:1-4.)

The spirit of God was poured out upon the waiting body at Pentecost. Such an empowering came after the return of Christ to be with his Father. The apostles stood in obedient, anxious expectation, and they were not to be disappointed.

Whenever the church, or one of its member congregations, to be more accurate, meets to conduct its affairs, it ought to be in the confident expectation that the Spirit of God will be its portion to guide and illumine. Some years ago Professor Philip Anderson published a book called *Church Meetings That Matter.* All of the meetings we conduct ought to matter; and if we allow God's presence to control us, they will.

PRAYER:

We thank you, Father, for your presence with us in this place tonight. We are gathered together to conduct your business. May the assurance of your power among us make our deliberations and means of help, comfort, and challenge to each person present. So may we be obedient to your claims over us.

In his name we pray.   Amen.

A Loving Fellowship (Philippians 1:1-11)

The salutation of the apostle Paul to the Philippians is an instructive one.

Paul has a totally untarnished memory of this church which he founded previously. In his daily prayers, many of which were made from a prison cell, he thanks God for their faith, that it has been strong and unwavering from the very time they heard the gospel preached. If you read some of the other letters of Paul, you will realize that not all his churches receive such commendation. Indeed, some have had squabbles and divisions, and the Apostle has had to reprimand them for their behavior.

What would the apostle Paul have to say were he writing to our church? Would he see it as a place of response, of an attitude of love one for the other, of growth in knowledge and discernment? We do not need to outline the realities but pledge ourselves to live as members of the Body of Christ so that our life together may be a glory to God and the means of proclaiming the gospel to our community.

PRAYER:

As we bow in your presence, O God, we ask that we may become more loving, more open to growth in Christian knowledge and discernment. Grant that our lives together may be marked by your indwelling and empowering. Make us your servant people.

We pray in the name of the Servant of all, Jesus Christ our Lord.

Amen.

True Worship of God (John 4:7-26)

The fourth chapter of John tells the story of the meeting of the woman from Samaria with Jesus at Jacob's well. As Jesus sat on the side of the well to rest, she came to draw water, and Jesus asked her for a drink.

(Read the conversation, verses 7-15, or 7-26 if time permits).

Out of this somewhat strange and enigmatic encounter come two or three memorable utterances that we could ponder. Jesus spoke of himself as the answer to the thirsts of the world for living water. The woman of Samaria seemed to understand and asked for some of this water. Then, as the conversation veered to discuss the proper place of worship, Jesus said: "But the hour is coming, and now is, when the true worshipers will worship the Father in spirit and truth, for such the Father seeks to worship him. God is spirit, and those who worship him must worship in spirit and truth" (John 4:23-24).

The essence of the church as a worshiping community is summed up in these few words. The Spirit of God is in our midst, and his truth keeps us free from error. The place of worship is unimportant; the mode and purpose are all-important.

Let us seek to honor God by allowing him to encounter us with his living presence, and let us put aside all lesser pursuits from our common life.

PRAYER:

We thirst, O God. Give us that drink so we thirst not again. We dwell in darkness and error; give us, then, we pray, your spirit and your truth. May we be open to all that you would give, and may it transform us to your honor and glory.

In Christ's name we ask it. Amen.

Meditations for Board and Committee Meetings

No Silver or Gold (Acts 3:1-10)

Have you ever stopped to ask yourself how many people passed that beggar at the gate of the temple, described in Acts 3:1-10, without helping him? Peter and John did not easily still the man's shouts by coolly tossing a coin in his direction. They stopped, found out his real need, and healed him.

Our world abounds with people along the roads and highways who are seeking for attention by one means or another. Not all of them wish to be saved, make no mistake about that. But many of them would be so pleased if one of us were to stop and ask, "What can I do to help?"

Don't stop if you are not sincere or if you are not prepared to listen and follow up. But if you are, there are thousands of persons who would love to be heard, really heard, and encountered at the point of their felt need. D. T. Niles used to define evangelism as "one beggar telling another where to find the bread."

Listen for the cries uttered along the highways of life, and in God's name respond to some of them. Silver and gold may not be nearly as important as what you have to offer.

PRAYER:

Keep us from putting people at arm's length by giving them silver and gold, O God. We know it is harder to give of ourselves and of our deep faith in you and your Son. Keep us from seeking the easy way out.

Through Christ we pray.   Amen.

Hear the Word of the Lord (Jeremiah 2:4, 13)

Two very pungent verses out of Jeremiah are worth pondering. "Hear the word of the Lord" is always a good maxim to observe. Then Jeremiah goes on to say on behalf of God:

> ". . . my people have committed two evils:
>   they have forsaken me,
> the fountain of living waters,
>   and hewed out cisterns for themselves,
> broken cisterns,
>   that can hold no water."

Since the beginning of time we have been prone to try to do our own will rather than God's. We have followed the words of men rather than those of God.

Sometimes we are inclined to gauge our piety by our prosperity (see Hebrews 3:17-19).

PRAYER:

Help us, O God, to listen to your voice and follow your will for our lives and churches. Help us to use your cisterns and use them to give needed water to a thirsty world.

In Christ we pray. Amen.

Meditations for Youth Meetings

True Wisdom (Proverbs 2:1-5)

It was Mark Twain, among others, who used to say that the only thing wrong with youth was that it came too early in life. Many people, looking back on their own youth, wish they could match the enthusiasm of youth with the experience life has taught them. The book of Proverbs is full of wise words but perhaps none more applicable than chapter 2, verses 1-5.

There is a tremendous store of knowledge available in our modern world. A high percentage of the physicists of all time are presently at work. We have opened up space and time, and the discoveries and exploits of our technology are ominous.

But what are we really about? What kind of a world are we truly interested in developing? What use is it to be able to communicate with the moon if people next door to each other don't speak?

True wisdom, such as Proverbs speaks about, relates us to God and his eternal purposes for our world and universe. It invites us to understand that there are more valuable things than the material, that God's ways are more durable than those of the world.

PRAYER:

Keep us, our Father, from being swallowed up by the temptation to confuse bigness with worth, or technology with value. Help us to know the wisdom that endures and the knowledge which will help us love you as our Father and our neighbors as ourselves.

In Christ's name we pray. Amen.

"Make My Name" (Acts 11:19-26)

A friend of ours worked in a day-care center in the Hyde Park area of Chicago. One day as he was working with the children, he helped one of the little boys cut his name out of construction paper. The boy then asked to have it pinned on his T-shirt. At five o'clock when his older sister came to take him home, he ran up to her and said, "See, this is who I am!"

He had learned to write his name, and in the process he had discovered something important about himself.

We read in the Acts of the Apostles that it was in Antioch that the followers of Jesus were first called "Christians." Probably at the beginning it was a nickname, maybe even a term of derision, but eventually the name stuck. (Read Acts 11:19-26.)

To be called a Christian is to have a name that denotes a relationship which is deep and abiding, one that tells the world who you really are. Wear the name responsibly and proudly.

PRAYER:

We thank you, our Father, that you have chosen us to be your children and allowed us to be your representatives in the world. May we bear your name faithfully and proudly in the world of your creation.

Through Christ we pray. Amen.

The Long View (Romans 8:26-28)

Sometimes we wonder about the way God runs his world. We can't explain earthquakes, tornadoes, epidemics, or other disasters; and our natural reaction is to question. At times such as these, it is even difficult for us to know how to pray. There are some helpful verses in Romans 8 (verses 26-28) which relate to this issue.

The Spirit of God indwells us and even helps us to pray. It keeps our prayers related to the will of God and prevents them from dwelling only on our desires or intents. When we are mired in the deepest distress, it is hardest to exercise faith and to pray. Then, says Romans, God helps us.

Ultimately, in the long view, God works things for our good. We may not understand how or when, but we are urged to believe and place our trust in God.

PRAYER:

Like Thomas of old, O God, we doubt and question those things that happen around us. We wonder about the suffering and torment of innocent people. Help us to understand that your way is the right way, and keep us faithful as your followers.

We ask in Christ's name.   Amen.

Meditations and Prayers Dealing with Social Concerns

Where Can I Find Eternal Life? (Mark 10:17-22)

There has always been a tension between private faith and social responsibility. A careful reading of the Gospels quickly shows us the deep concern that Jesus had for all persons and particularly for those who were poor, who lacked status or power, or who had no one to champion their cause. He took the part of the underdog. One of the most interesting episodes is that of the rich young man who came to Jesus with the question: "Good Teacher, what must I do to inherit eternal life?" (See Mark 10:17-22.)

Jesus emphasized the necessity for relating private faith to social concern, and the young man was seemingly unable to throw over his wealth in order to help the poor. We do not know that he ever returned to seek out the Master.

The question before us is one that never goes away. What is God requiring of us and what are those things in our lives that might keep us from a complete obedience to him?

PRAYER:

We live in a privileged part of the world, our Father, and we are deeply grateful to you for all your blessings to us. However, we would ask that the good things of life not stand between us and the giving of a better account of our stewardship to you. If we are failing to do what you would have us do, reveal it to us and help us to do it.

In your name we pray.   Amen.

———————

PRAYER:

Keep our eyes and ears open, our Father, to the needs of the community around us. As we share the crust of bread with the hungry and the cup of water with those who thirst, help us also to be concerned about the causes of the hunger and thirst.

In your name and for your sake may we seek not to be served but to serve.   Amen.

PRAYER:

All around us people are oppressed, are treated badly because of color, race, or condition. Forgive us, our Father, for the part we have played in those acts of dishonor. Give us the vision and the strength to reverse and correct the conditions that brought about oppression. Give us the ability to know and practice the loving of our neighbors as ourselves.

Through Christ we pray.   Amen.

————————————

PRAYER:

We pause at the beginning of our meeting to acknowledge your goodness to us. We would be faithful stewards of your inheritance. Help us to share our resources and ourselves with those around us to the end so that the love with which you have loved us may be known abroad. Send us forth into the community knowing that we never go alone.

In Christ's name we ask.   Amen.

2

SANCTUARY WORSHIP

The lay person's role in sanctuary worship has usually been restricted to the reading of the Scriptures—thus, the term "lay reader." The only requirement for this is to read carefully the selection beforehand since very seldom is the lay reader required to select the passage. Thus, the role is not much more than a token one and requires little more than the ability to read publicly.

We suggest that lay participation in the service can and should fall more into a leadership category. Without suggesting that the minister abdicate all authority or leadership, we think those appointed by the congregation to work with the minister in the worship service should do more than just follow directions. This would also mean that special talents within the congregation could be used and encouraged.

Poetry is one of those talents available within the congregation, and if tied to an understanding of the Christian faith, there are a number of ways that it can be used within the service: calls to worship, invocation prayers, other prayers, benedictions, and offertories. The poet may write only for others, or he or she may read his or her work within the service as well.

Music plays a large role within the service. The music director, choir director, and organist all have talents to be encouraged, and each one should be in dialogue with the minister in preparing a service. The choice of hymns, anthems, solos, and musical worship aids should be considered as important as any other part of the service in the sanctuary and not left to a "hope it fits" type of planning. The choir and soloists should be regarded as leaders in worship. Their talents and suggestions are important. Perhaps a meeting of all the leaders and participants in worship should be held at least twice a year to discuss and share ideas about worship and how each person might give leadership.

As a member of the church, you can use your talents in a spiritual way by standing before the people and humbly giving what you have to God. If you can sew and have an artistic bent, fabric graphics can "speak" very significantly within the context of worship. Though there has been a tendency to think of cut-out felt banners as Sunday school room decoration, the church has for many years draped from pulpit, communion table, and walls various fabrics with symbols upon them identifying the function or theme of the season or meaning of a worship experience. This kind of expression can add a great deal to a service. Art can be translated to worship program folders. Translating themes of worship into symbols or even photographs for this use can bring a focus to worship that deepens the meaning of the act. Ways to use fabric graphics and art effectively in worship are discussed further in chapter 7.

The reader will notice that we have included in this section several worship resources couched in the "King James idiom." We have done this for several reasons. For many people this is still the most natural and acceptable form in which worship ought to be offered to Almighty God. Also, many of the examples included have been contributed by lay persons for inclusion in services of worship. They were used, and they provided a very fine vehicle of expression to the congregation. A congregation's receiving such an offering in worship from one of its members adds a personal dimension of life that speaks to the essential community of faith which is gathered for worship and praise.

We include varying forms of worship to encourage all leaders of worship to use the forms most natural to themselves and to those to whom they give leadership in worship. We want things to be done decently and in good order, of course, but the more easily prayer, benediction, and litany is understood, the more completely can one participate and make it one's own. Almost all of the material in this section has come out of the worship experience of local congregations.

Prayers (In Unison)

Open our hearts, O God. We seek not to escape from the world but to see it in a new way and in seeing to understand. We come together with questions, but we do not know how to share. We come also to celebrate, but the anxiety of our daily lives overcomes us. Renew in us now, O God, the strength to let your demands upon us live in our hearts and the peace to celebrate in compassion, openness, and joy.
Through Christ we ask.   Amen.

Christ, thou wert the servant of all life,
bowing thine holiness to our strife.
Teach us to serve, like thee, with all mind and breath,
submitting, only never unto final death.

Lord, we come before thee with our pride
held tightly around our soul that we may hide
from the necessity of thy truth and sight.
Make us thy servants, humbled in thy light.

Prayers of Supplication (In Unison)

Have mercy on me, O God, according to your steadfast love; according to your abundant mercy, blot out my transgressions. Wash me thoroughly from my iniquity, and cleanse me from my sin. For I know my transgressions, and my sin is ever before me. Against you, you only, have I sinned and done that which is evil in your sight so that you are justified in your sentence and blameless in your judgment.   Amen.

Help us, O God, to live as those who are prepared to die. And then, when thy summons comes, help us to die as those who go forth to live so that, living or dying, our life may be hidden with Christ in thee, and nothing henceforth in life or in death will be able to separate us from thy great love which is in Christ Jesus our Lord.   Amen.

A Prayer for the New Year (In Unison)

O God, in the midst of the fears and frustrations that haunt us in this year's beginning, help us to show intelligence, compassion, peace, and poise. Help us to face the future with courage and commitment, sensitive to human need, disciplined in our opportunities, and patient in times of failure. Teach us, day by day, new ways to ground our lives in your unmoving love.

Grant us serenity to accept the things we cannot change, courage to change the things we can, wisdom to know the difference.

Above all, meet with us and reveal yourself to us in all we do.

Through Jesus Christ our Lord we pray.   Amen.

Declaration of God's Goodness (Psalm 100)

LEADER: Make a joyful noise to the Lord, all the lands!

PEOPLE: Serve the Lord with gladness! Come into his presence with singing!

LEADER: Know that the Lord is God! It is he that made us, and we are his;

PEOPLE: We are his people, and the sheep of his pasture.

LEADER: Enter his gates with thanksgiving, and his courts with praise!

PEOPLE: Give thanks to him, bless his name!

LEADER: For the Lord is good; his steadfast love endures for ever,

PEOPLE: And his faithfulness to all generations.

Sentences for the Opening of Worship

"Ask, and you will receive; seek, and you will find; knock, and the door will be opened. For everyone who asks receives, he who seeks finds, and to him who knocks, the door will be opened" (Matthew 7:7-8, NEB).

Let your bearing towards one another arise out of your life in Christ Jesus. For the divine nature was his from the first; yet he did not think to snatch at equality with God, but made himself nothing, assuming the nature of a slave. Bearing the human likeness, revealed in human shape, he humbled himself, and in obedience accepted even death—death on a cross. Therefore God raised him to the heights and bestowed on him the name above all names, that at the name of Jesus every knee should bow—in heaven, on earth, and in the depths—and every tongue confess, "Jesus Christ is Lord," to the glory of God the Father (Philippians 2:5-11, NEB).

———————

Our help is in the name of the Lord, who made heaven and earth (Psalm 124:8).

———————

O come, let us worship and bow down, let us kneel before the Lord, our Maker! For he is our God, and we are the people of his pasture, and the sheep of his hand (Psalm 95:6-7).

———————

Know that the Lord is God! It is he that made us, and we are his; we are his people, and the sheep of his pasture (Psalm 100:3).

———————

It is good to give thanks to the Lord, to sing praises to thy name, O Most High; to declare thy steadfast love in the morning, and thy faithfulness by night . . . (Psalm 92:1-2).

———————

> Though the fig tree do not blossom,
>   nor fruit be on the vines,
> the produce of the olive fail
>   and the fields yield no food,
> the flock be cut off from the fold
>   and there be no herd in the stalls,
> yet I will rejoice in the Lord,
>   I will joy in the God of my salvation.
> God, the Lord, is my strength;
>   he makes my feet like hinds' feet,
>   he makes me tread upon my high places.
>   Habakkuk 3:17-19

———————

"Seek the Lord while he may be found,
  call upon him while he is near;
let the wicked forsake his way,

and the unrighteous man his thoughts;
let him return to the Lord, that he may have mercy on him,
and to our God, for he will abundantly pardon."

Isaiah 55:6-7

"But the time approaches, indeed it is already here, when those who are real worshippers will worship the Father in spirit and in truth. Such are the worshippers whom the Father wants. God is spirit, and those who worship him must worship in spirit and in truth" (John 4:23-24, NEB).

Invocations

Lord, renew thy light.
Ignite hope in our learning and faith in our prayers.
Give us love in our foolishness, forgiveness for our sin.

MINISTER: We are the children of humankind,
Created by the hand of God.
PEOPLE: For as in Adam all die,
Even so in Christ shall all be made alive.
MINISTER: Death is the gift of God to all humankind
That we might truly see God face to face.
PEOPLE: For as in Adam all die,
Even so in Christ shall all be made alive.
MINISTER: Without any meaning would be death or eternity
Without the mercy and forgiveness of Christ.
ALL: Christ, Savior of all the world,
Have mercy upon us.

O Lord, where our thoughts have turned away
To hide in the shadows and the night,
With gentle power take our groping hand—
Turn us to face thine infinite light.

We come before thy presence

Bringing eternity with us;
May we make the commitment
To open our eyes
To thy love.

Offertory Prayers and Words

O Lord, we have been scattered like sheep and have walked in paths far from our own comfort. Return us, then, to that true home for which we long—the joy of the knowledge of thy presence.   Amen.

——————

As thou hast shown us the light of thy glorious love, strengthen our weak flame that we may move through darkness with love and mercy as our lamp.   Amen.

——————

That love which fills our soul with peace
Calls us to action of deed and mind
To serve with our energies for God
And grapple with the truth to learn and find.

——————

O Lord, teach us to return our mind's thoughts, our body's energies, our soul's yearning—all to thee. We have received them, thy free gifts.   Amen.

——————

We bring these gifts of your worshiping people, O God, and return them to you out of gratitude for your generous love to us. May these gifts represent our larger giving of life, time, talents, and love.
In the name of Christ we pray.   Amen.

——————

Our gifts are laid upon your altar, O God. In this act of giving we would present ourselves to you as the only sacrifice really worth giving. May our lives continually be given to your service even as our Lord Jesus gave his life for us.
In his name and for his sake we pray.   Amen.

Communion Prayers

General

We give thanks, our Father, that you have provided us tangible reminders of your self-giving to us in Christ Jesus. We tend to forget. In these pieces of broken bread and this cup we see the broken body of our Lord and the blood shed for the salvation of the world. May we come to your table with a sense of humility and self-giving that we may receive all the blessings you have in store for us. We confess our unworthiness, but you can make us worthy.

In that hope we come in the name of Jesus.   Amen.

"Take, eat; this is my body, broken. . . . Drink of it all of you." We contemplate the total sacrifice required to make these invitations possible. Our hearts are filled with gratitude and wonder that you have loved us as you have. As we stretch forth our hands to receive your gifts, may we dedicate our total lives in grateful service. Nothing less can match your care for your children.

Hear us; through Christ we pray.   Amen.

We would remember, O God, that your Son was not crucified on a golden cross carefully set between two candles on a table but on a hill outside the city. We would also remember, as we take bread and wine into our mouths, that it is the body of Christ broken and his blood spilled that we commemorate.

Purge us from all self-righteous and false estimates of worth. Help us to stand before your table to receive your blessing and salvation.

In the name of Christ we ask.   Amen.

For the Bread

You said: "I am the bread of life." Before us we have bread broken, symbolizing your body broken in self-giving for the salvation of the world. May we look beyond the bread in our hands to the life-giving presence you offer, and may we never more hunger.

In the name of Jesus Christ we pray.   Amen.

"Take, eat; this is my body, broken." Those words prompt us to quiet meditation and adoration. May they also prompt us, this very day, to a greater sense of dedication to the Christ who counted not the cost but gave himself for the redemption of the world.   Amen.

———————

Bread means life. It sustains us and gives health and strength day in and day out. Now we see bread on your table. Speak to us in this visible sign of the spiritual life and strength you offer to us in your Son, our Savior.

May we eat in humble dependence upon your grace, we pray.
                                                                                    Amen.

For the Cup

"This cup is the new covenant." Today on your table, our Father, we see tangible proof of your constant love for us. Even when persons spurned your covenant and turned their backs to you, you sent your Son to continue loving us. May we never fail to give ourselves in gratitude to you.

We ask in his name.   Amen.

———————

Draw near to us again, O God, in these visible signs of your self-giving. We remember the cost which made this cup possible. As we drink, may it be the means of nourishing in us a gratitude and devotion made possible by your power.

Through Christ we pray.   Amen.

———————

"Do this, as often as you drink it, in remembrance of me." We give heartfelt thanks that you have bidden us come to your table so that we do not forget. You have loved us. Your self-giving is most evident in the cross. May the memory strengthen us to give more of ourselves to you.

We ask in Christ.   Amen.

Prayers of the People

Probably one of the hardest parts of a service of worship to prepare is the "prayer of the people." We have deliberately used this term because some of the terms now used to describe this portion of our worship do not provoke strong, helpful responses. We do not want to call it the "pastoral prayer" because then it is misunderstood by many as being the pastor's prayer (this is clearly not what it was intended to be), nor do we want to call it the "long prayer," although many worshipers find it to be this no matter how many minutes' duration.

It ought to be—really, must be—an attempt to offer in the service of worship a prayer of all the persons assembled. Admittedly, this is no mean task. It is quite clear that not every prayer will reflect invariably the mood of every worshiper, but there are a number of common concerns that all share.

In almost every family there are those who are ill or whose health is, at best, precarious. There are births, weddings, graduations, employments, promotions, deaths, and separations. There are sorrows, frustrations, aspirations, and decisions to be made at every juncture of life. Add these to the need for growth in our knowledge of God, our need to have wavering faith renewed, our need for forgiveness and reconciliation. Also, we have deep concerns for those who suffer—the depressed; the oppressed; victims of pestilence, storm, earthquake, and fire. All of these and more are the shared concerns of an average congregation when it gathers for worship on the Lord's Day.

Many leaders of worship have found that they can be most helpful to a congregation by dividing the prayers into their "natural" liturgical divisions and interspersing them throughout the service. Prayers of thanksgiving, intercession, penitence or pardon, dedication, supplication, and illumination, can be included, as well as prayers for grace, and offertory prayers. In the use of these more abbreviated prayers the leader is consciously giving the worshipers more specific instruction and foreknowledge concerning the subject matter of prayers and invites the worshiper to a more ready participation. Hopefully, the focus will be clearer and the tendency to wander lessened by such changes in the order of the worship.

Prayers of the people should be just that—not someone's private prayers offered in public or an austere, distinct kind of spiritual exercise which leaves the worshiper as a spectator or, even worse, as a questioning outsider who cannot really decide what he or she is supposed to be doing at that moment.

Prayers of Approach

O God, like the psalmist of old we come to give thanks unto you with our whole hearts. We come to your house to thank you for your steadfast love, your faithfulness in all of our days. Even though you are exalted above all things, you hear our voice and you answer us when we cry unto you. Draw near unto us again, we pray, and help us to offer you a perfect worship.

Through Christ we pray.   Amen.

We praise the name of the Lord in the house of the Lord, in the courts of the house of the Lord. We sing praises to the name of our Lord, for he is gracious. You have chosen us for yourself, O Lord, and we come to adore and worship your holy name. As we contemplate your creative power, may we also feel your compassion and love and respond in self-giving love to you.

In the name of Jesus who gave his all we pray.   Amen.

Prayer of Confession

Out of the depths do we cry unto you, O Lord, for you are attentive to the voice of our supplications; your ears hear our cry. If you, O Lord, did not forgive, who could stand before you? But there is forgiveness with you, and we confess our sin. As you did redeem Israel from all iniquities, so grant us your steadfast love. May we live as your redeemed people for the sake of our blessed Lord who brought us to yourself.   Amen.

Prayer of Thanksgiving

"O give thanks to the Lord, for he is good; his steadfast love endures forever." We come again, O God, to offer unto you our grateful praise for all of your blessings to us. You have created, sustained, redeemed, and loved us in so many ways. We have not always acknowledged your grace in our lives, but at this moment we pause to say a thank-you. May we continue in this grace as our lives extol you and as we seek in all we do to reflect gratitude and thanksgiving to you, the giver of all. For your goodness and steadfast love that endure forever, we give you our thanks.   Amen.

Prayers of Intercession

Father, you have not created us to live alone, nor have you made us all alike. We pray for our families where our lives are lived that they may be places of love, support, and faith. When we quarrel, help us to find it possible quickly to forgive; when we are impatient, teach us the meaning of concern. Be with us where we work. Infuse all places of labor with a sense of dignity and purpose that we may have the sense of well-being that comes from knowing we are worthy of our hire.

May our communities be places of support for all good citizens so that all men may be free to live in conscience and responsibility.

May peace and justice come to all peoples.

Through Christ we pray.   Amen.

We remember before you this day, our Father, those who carry heavy burdens alone—some are sick and in pain; some bear the troubles of families plagued by disease and disruption; some are carrying a load of guilt and sin and are staggering to find relief; some have lost their ways in the dark and need direction.

For these and all others in stress we ask your gentle and gracious intervention. Draw them nearer to yourself and give unto them the blessing you know they need. If it be your will, use us even as we pray as your agents of reconciliation in your world.

In Christ's name we ask.   Amen.

Prayer for Senior's Sunday

Our loving heavenly Father, we come to you on this special day to give thanks for your continuing goodness to your children. Over many years you have guided us and shown us your salvation. Your forgiveness has enabled us to forgive; your redemption teaches us to be redemptive; your love teaches us to love.

In spite of all your providence we have failed and done that which is evil in your sight. Even in our advancing years we would learn afresh the meaning of your pardoning grace.

We give thanks for every child of yours who has brought enrichment and new life into our living. For godly parents, tried and true examples, for those who have sustained and supported us, for those who have been demanding of us, for all these we give our grateful praise.

Help us to overcome life's little problems and to know that you are ever ready to be our guide and counselor. May we be able to say in the evening time of life that we walked with God and that our Father walked with us.

Hear us in the name of Jesus Christ, who taught us to call you our Father.   Amen.

Seasonal Prayers

There are times and seasons both in the Christian year and in nature that stimulate the most natural and spontaneous expression of prayer. Who can fail to be grateful to God that "seedtime and harvest do not fail" or that the whole world emerges from the depths of winter to burst again into color and life?

Easter, Advent, Thanksgiving, Pentecost, all of these and many more will suggest a natural ordering for your leadership in worship. Not all denominations rely upon the church year for the ordering of their worship, but there are a tremendous number of excellent resources among those denominational groups that do. We are suggesting the following as a catalyst for you. Look around and allow your own observations to guide you in expressing to God the way you feel, and allow yourself to join with the countless thousands of those who across the centuries have expressed their adoration, thanksgiving, petition, or whatever in cadence with the changing year.

The Christian year presents many festivals around which the worship of the church is gathered, for example, Christmas, Easter, Pentecost. There are also seasonal times of national celebration, such as Thanksgiving and memorial days around which we can center our worship. The changes of the seasons that take place in a large part of North America also make us aware of the constancy of God's creation and of the dependency of the world in which we live.

One of the most obvious advantages of seasonal worship is that you are given a ready entrée into the worshipers' life situations. Few, indeed, are the people who are totally unaware of the breaking out of new life in a world that has been hidden under a blanket of snow for several months. Rare, also, is the person who cannot naturally rejoice when nature clothes itself in the riotous colors of the autumn season and the whole world seems to present itself in "Kodachrome."

This is the time when visuals of one kind or another lend themselves so well to the leading of worship experiences. Even a single picture or slide can focus on a particularly spectacular example of nature's beauty and help a group of people to center on an attitude of worship. A series of slides or a well-chosen filmstrip backed by an appropriate piece of music is another way of providing a bridge from one mood to another. In young people's or children's gatherings, particularly those held out-of-doors, one of the most natural and meaningful ways of providing this transition is by the use of songs. As one moves from the rollicking secular kind of songs to the more meditative kind of music, a mood is established which almost demands worship. Most of us have happy memories of late evening campfires at camp when worship seemed so natural and when the presence of God seemed so near.

In Spring

The world is unfolding itself and breaking forth into life. The greens and the other colors of flowers gladden heart and eye. We are reminded that all life comes from your hand, and we give you grateful thanks. May we be as responsive to the light of your love as the bulb is when it responds to the heat of the sun. May we bring forth fruits of loving service even as the beauty of nature comes to delight our lives.

In Christ we pray.   Amen.

In Summer

Your constant provision for us, O God, reminds us of your creative love and care for the world. We have so much for which to be grateful. Help us to develop grateful hearts so that we will show our gratitude to all with whom we come in touch. Remind us, too, that others in our world do not have enough to eat; help us to share our bounty with them. May we never look upon your gifts as a right, but always as a part of your grace.   Amen.

In Autumn

The fields have yielded their increase, and we have taken in another bountiful harvest. Seedtime and harvest have not failed; your constancy is ever with us. For all of your good gifts we give hearty thanks, our Father. May we also seek to store up in our minds and hearts such treasures of your grace that will help us live through the days before us. May we then share these good gifts with our families, friends, and all who need our love.

In Christ's name we pray.   Amen.

In Winter

Snow covers the ground, O God, and we know that it provides warmth to the earth as well as beauty to the eye. In this time of resting and cold, help us to keep alive the powers of your love in our hearts, for these need never die.

As we seek the fire for warmth, so may we, your children together, also provide warmth and love to all we meet that they may know that we are yours and come to know you, too, the God and Father of our Lord Jesus in whose name we pray.   Amen.

Prayer for a New Day

Another day stretches before us like sand newly washed by the waves. No foot has disturbed it for as far as the eye can see. One sees it almost like an invitation to a journey.

Come, let us walk through the hours of this day confident of new experiences and of new encounters with friends and those we've never met, confident that God will guide us in our every step and keep us from all wrong. Let us see the day as a new challenge to live.

O God, we pause to thank you for life. Make the hours of this day a time of challenge, of joy, and of meeting. Help us through the easy and the hard moments. May we be assured that you are always with us.

In the name of your Son we pray.   Amen.

At Day's End

Many thoughts stream into our consciousness as we look back on another day: the happiness, the sorrow, the piques and frustrations, the opportunities to help and comfort. All of these fly across our memories. God has been good to us in the gift of life; we examine our stewardship of this gift.

Our Father, as the sun sinks below the horizon and beckons us to sleep, we pause to give thanks for today. Accept our labors as an offering placed on your altar. Forgive our faults, our sins, our laziness. Be with all whom we've met this day and help them to know the true rest that comes from your presence.

In Christ's name we pray.   Amen.

Thoughts and Prayers of Great Christians

It is all too easy to get in a rut when praying. Even when we use the prayer which our blessed Lord gave to us, we sometimes rattle it off quickly and carelessly. One way to add depth and meaning to our prayer expression is to read the prayers and thoughts of others and allow them to express our own hopes, aspirations, and affirmations. In the same way as the hymn writers help us sing praise to God, so these thoughts can facilitate our spoken praise.

We are suggesting prayer forms which have helped us in our expressions of prayer to God and are doing so to point to the vast resources available. Some of the greatest prayers are couched in traditional or even archaic language, and you may wish to translate these into modern form. In any case, the essence is there, and we suggest you dig it out and benefit from it.

Albert Schweitzer

Both great and small personages tend to forget to say a thank-you for benefits received. The renowned missionary-musician-doctor reminds us to be grateful enough to say, "Thank you." Perhaps if we all thought of the times we have received favors from our family, our friends, and our acquaintances, we would use those magic words more often—"Thank you."

Luke 17:11-19 tells the story alluded to by Dr. Schweitzer. Rereading it will bring new light to the old story and help you to a new appreciation.

DAY 45   *Say Thank You*

When I look back upon my early days I am stirred by the thought of the number of people whom I have to thank for what they gave me or for what they were to me. At the same time I am haunted by an oppressive consciousness of the little gratitude I really showed them when I was young. . . . For all that, I think I can say with truth that I am not ungrateful. I did occasionally wake up out of that youthful thoughtlessness. . . . But down to my twentieth year, and even later still, I did not exert myself sufficiently to express the gratitude which was really in my heart. I valued too low the pleasure I felt at receiving real proofs of gratitude. Often, too, shyness prevented me from expressing the gratitude I felt.

As a result of this experience with myself I refuse to think that there is so much ingratitude in the world as is commonly maintained. I have never interpreted the parable of the Ten Lepers to mean that only one was grateful. All the ten, surely, were grateful, but nine of them hurried home first . . . One of them, however, had a disposition which made him act at once as his feelings bade him; he sought out the person who had helped him, and refreshed his soul with the assurance of his gratitude.

In the same way we ought all to make an effort to act on our first thoughts and let our unspoken gratitude find expression. Then there will be more sunshine in the world, and more power to work for what is good. But as concerns ourselves, we must all of us take care not to adopt as part of a theory of life all people's bitter sayings about the ingratitude of the world. A great deal of water is flowing underground which never comes up as a spring. In that thought we may find comfort. But we ourselves must try to be the water which does find its way up; we must become a spring at which men can quench their thirst for gratitude.

                                                          Albert Schweitzer [1]

[1] John Baillie, *A Diary of Readings* (London: Oxford University Press, 1957).

John Wesley

The story of the reawakening of John Wesley can be the source of inspiration for you and your group as it has for thousands over the last century. It speaks of John Wesley's heart "being strangely warmed"—a lovely phrase to describe a person's encounter with the Spirit of God. The experience of Wesley can bring warmth into our cold, calculating world and perhaps help each of us to experience the same kind of strength which enabled John Wesley to become such a stalwart servant of God.

DAY 73 *John Wesley's Heart Strangely Warmed*

I think it was about five this morning that I opened my Testament on those words, "There are given unto us exceeding great and precious promises, even that ye should be partakers of the divine nature." Just as I went out, I opened it again on those words, "Thou art not far from the kingdom of God." In the afternoon I was asked to go to St. Paul's. The anthem was, "Out of the deep have I called unto thee, O Lord. O let thine ears consider well the voice of my complaint. If thou, Lord, wilt be extreme to mark what is done amiss, O Lord, who may abide it? For there is mercy with thee; therefore shalt thou be feared, O Israel, trust in the Lord: for with the Lord there is mercy, and with him is plenteous redemption. And he shall redeem Israel from all his sins."

In the evening I went very unwillingly to a society in Aldersgate Street, where one was reading Luther's preface to the Epistle to the Romans. About a quarter before nine, while he was describing the change which God works in the heart through faith in Christ, I felt my heart strangely warmed. I felt I did trust in Christ, Christ alone, for my salvation; and an assurance was given me that He had taken away my sins, even mine, and saved me from the law of sin and death.

I began to pray with all my might for those who had in a more especial manner despitefully used me and persecuted me. I then testified openly to all there what I now first felt in my heart. But it was not long before the enemy suggested, "This cannot be faith; for where is thy joy?" Then was I taught that peace and victory over sin are essential to faith in the Captain of our salvation; but that, as to the transports of joy that usually attend the beginning of it, especially in those who have mourned deeply, God sometimes giveth, sometimes withholdeth them, according to the counsels of His own will.

John Wesley[2]

S. Weiss

A prayer of the eighteenth century is entitled "A Prayer for Illumination." In the simplest of terms, old-fashioned as they are, the petitioner, Weiss, lifts his soul before God in earnest seeking. Out of

[2] *Ibid.*

the darkness surrounding him he asks for light. It brings to mind the familiar saying "Better to light a candle than curse the darkness."

Many of Jesus' sayings spoke of light. Take another look at Matthew 5:14-16 and see if these words do not shed more illumination for you in addition to the words of Weiss.

A Prayer for Illumination

Father, thou knowest that alone we can do nothing. Behold, we seek thee, but of ourselves we cannot find thee; we long for thy light, but we cannot illuminate our own souls; we desire thy grace, but alone we cannot win it; we know thy will, but without thy support we are unable to fulfil it. Help us, therefore, since we cannot help ourselves; send down thy Spirit into our hearts so that whatever we do may be done to thy glory; may he purify, enlighten, strengthen and sanctify us.

Let not thy word have been spoken in vain to us, and grant that we may be not hearers only, but doers of the same, and that it may bring forth the true fruits of salvation in our hearts. Turn not thy face from us, and withdraw not thy grace; lead us ever in the right way, and let thy Holy Spirit encourage us; may we never sink back into darkness, nor into error, but let the light of thy life shine on us evermore. Teach us to do according to thy pleasure, and take not away thy good Spirit from us.

Amen.[3]

Brother Lawrence

The main work of Brother Lawrence is called by the rather strange title *The Practice of the Presence of God*. It is a practice that sounds rather odd to modern ears, and yet the message he brings is ever modern.

It is the firm conviction of the good brother that it is not God who has fled from us, but we who have excluded God from our lives.

Sometimes we tend to think that God is far from us. Not so says Brother Lawrence. "I wish you could convince yourself that God is often nearer to us, and more effectually present with us, in sickness than in health."

The psalmist was affirming a similar confidence in Psalm 23. Even the deepest deep or the blackest night does not separate the believer from God nor quench hope.

DAY 302   *The Practice of the Presence of God*

Those whose spirits are stirred by the breath of the Holy Spirit go forward even in sleep.

•   •   •

[3] S. Weiss, *A Book of Prayers for Students* (London: SCM, 1915), pp. 85-86.

You need not cry very loud: He is nearer to us than we think.

> •   •   •

I hope that when I have done what I can, He will do with me what He pleases.

> •   •   •

There is need neither of art nor of science for going to God, but only a heart resolutely determined to apply itself to nothing but Him, or for His sake, and to love Him only.

> •   •   •

A little lifting up of the heart suffices; a little remembrance of God, one act of inward worship, though upon a march and sword in hand, are prayers which, however short, are nevertheless very acceptable to God; and far from lessening a soldier's courage, they best serve to fortify it.

> •   •   •

One way to recall easily the mind in time of prayer, and to preserve it more in rest, is not to let it wander too far at other times. You should keep it strictly in the Presence of God, and being accustomed to think of Him often from time to time, you will find it easy to keep your mind calm in time of prayer, or at least to recall it from its wanderings.

> •   •   •

I wish you could convince yourself that God is often nearer to us, and more effectually present with us, in sickness than in health.

Brother Lawrence[4]

Prayer of St. Patrick

> I pray for the power of God to guide me,
> The might of God to uphold me,
> The wisdom of God to teach me,
> The eye of God to watch over me,
> The ear of God to hear me,
> The word of God to give me speech,
> The hand of God to guide me,
> The shield of God to shelter me,
> The host of God to protect me.
> Christ be with me,
> Christ before me, Christ behind me,
> Christ within me, Christ below me, Christ above me,
> Christ at my right hand, Christ at my left,
> Christ in the heart of every man that thinks of me,
> Christ in the mouth of every man that speaks of me,
> In every eye that sees me,
> In every ear that hears me.

Amen.[5]

---

[4] Baille, *op. cit.*

[5] A modification of a prayer of St. Patrick from J. F. Fox, *A Chain of Prayers Across the Ages* (London: John Murray Ltd., 1913), p. 65.

So much is highlighted in the prayer of the saint—the love of God, the providence of God, the inner-dwelling of God with his people, the fact that God goes with us everywhere and we are never outside his love and care. Let us seek in our prayers to practice the presence of God, to allow him to act in our lives as we follow his Christ and listen for his Spirit.

Prayer of John Baillie

I would pray tonight, O God, for all those souls and conditions of men to whom Jesus Christ was wont to give especial thought and care,
For those lacking in food or drink or raiment;
For the sick and all who are wasted by disease;
For the blind;
For the maimed and the lame;
For lepers;
For prisoners;
For those oppressed by any injustice;
For the lost sheep of our human society;
For fallen women;
For all lonely strangers within our gates;
For the worried and anxious;
For those who are living faithful lives in obscurity;
For those who are fighting bravely in unpopular causes;
For all who are laboring diligently in Thy vineyard.[6]

Jesus seemed most interested in the least, the last, and the lost. This prayer which lists so many of those whom Jesus touched reminds us of the people of our society who still need to be touched in the strong name of Jesus.

Take time to reflect on some of those around you who may reach out to you and pray that you will have the cup of water, the crust of bread, the word of comfort, whatever they need when that time comes.

John W. Taylor

Reflect for a moment on the prayers you have heard. How few of them include a plea for humility, to be enabled to use the common, everyday gifts which are so readily at our disposal. To offer simple hospitality to the stranger is such a gift. John W. Taylor helps us to a renewed perspective and perhaps a new avenue of service.

[6] John Baillie, *A Diary of Private Prayer* (London: Oxford Press, 1958), p. 59.

DAY 79   *The Doorkeeper*

To keep God's door—
I am not fit.
I would not ask for more
Than this—
    To stand or sit
Upon the threshold of God's House
Out of the reach of sin,
To open wide His door
To those who come,
To welcome Home
His children and His poor:
To wait and watch
The gladness on the face of those
That are within:
Sometimes to catch
A glimpse or trace of those
I love the best, and know
That all I failed to be,
And all I failed to do,
Has not sufficed
To bar them from the Tree
of Life, the Paradise of God,
The Face of Christ.
                    John W. Taylor[7]

PRAYER:

Transform the common experiences of life, our Father, into instruments of your blessing. May we never lose the close opportunities for living because of looking beyond to the distant dreams.

In Christ's name we pray.   Amen.

[7] Baillie, *A Diary of Readings*.

3

RESOURCES FOR ADVENT

Call to Worship and Offertory Words

First Sunday in Advent

Call to Worship: "The Conception"
        'Tis Advent season,
        Lord, open our hearts for thee
        That we may be pure,
        Acceptable in thy sight
        To receive thy grace through Christ.
Offertory Word:
        Christ came into the world as God's gift of love.
        Our gift of love can be nothing less than ourselves.

Second Sunday in Advent

Call to Worship: "The Testimony of the Scriptures"
        Come, Emmanuel,
        As thy prophets have foretold;
        May we hear their words
        With joy renewed in our minds!
        Christ, be born again in us.

Offertory Word:

> If we call Christ to be reborn in us, does that
> Mean we will give of ourselves as Christ gave?

Third Sunday in Advent

Call to Worship: "Prepare Ye the Way"

> Lord, as thou didst send
> A voice in the wilderness:
> "Prepare ye the way,"
> Move the mountains of our pride;
> Humble our souls for thy birth.

Offertory Word:

> God of all giving,
> we have seen your way
> and heard your voice in the
> wildernesses of life. Hear us
> now in Thanksgiving as we
> present our offerings
> unto you.

Fourth Sunday in Advent

Call to Worship: "The Birth"

> Jesus, born a child
> To be crucified for humankind,
> One God forever,
> May we kneel at thy cradle
> As before thy glorious throne.

Offertory Word:

> We kneel in adoration and devotion
> before the cradle of the Savior.
> We too bring gifts: of heart, mind, soul and
> spirit, represented in these tangible gifts.

Meditations for Advent

I Couldn't Care Less

How many times have we heard someone say, "I couldn't care less"? It is a common saying and unfortunately reflects a great deal of the detachment and anonymity of our civilization.

The message of the Advent couldn't be more counter to this sentiment. What the message of this season is saying is, "I couldn't care more."

The appearance of the *star* signified the beginning of a brand new era.

The birth of the *Child* signified the beginning of a new and radical revolution.

The response of the *wise men* signified the beginning of a new openness.

God says to the world, "I couldn't care more." The question posed to us is clear: "What do we care about?"

The world of our day needs care, deep and costly care that responds to human need wherever it is discovered. Where there are cries, the hearing person hears and responds.

SCRIPTURE: Luke 2:1-20.

PRAYER: The Nunc Dimittis (Luke 2:29-32).

Good News at Christmas

The church has always cherished the "servant passages" of Isaiah as most beautifully depicting the meaning of Christ's coming to earth. Isaiah 42:1-4 is a poetic description of the Lord's servant who will come. He has been specially chosen of God to come to a heedless and disobedient world to bring good news. As we now know all too well, bearers of good news are frequently misunderstood, abused, even put out of the way. However, in spite of all this, the Servant will persevere and the message will be proclaimed. Let us pray in silence as we are directed:

> O God, speak again to us the good news of your
> salvation.
> As the Child comes into our midst, may we
> hear your Servant.
> Forgive, we pray, the occasions in our time
> when we have caused your servant pain, when
> we have turned our backs upon him in stony
> silence.
> Establish justice and peace on the earth. We
> pray for all persons who suffer from humanity's cruel
> treatment of one another.
> In the little baby of Christmas, may we see your
> message of giving love, and may we seek to give

in return to all whom we meet.

> In the name of the Child who
> grew to become our Savior and
> Lord we pray.
>
> Amen.

Peace at Christmas

One of the recurring themes of Christmas is that of peace, the angels' song of peace on earth, of goodwill to all people. Away back in the time of Isaiah, the prophet looked anxiously for a time when persons would submit their ways to God and allow peace to reign in their lives. "He shall judge between the nations, and shall decide for many peoples; and they shall beat their swords into ploughshares, and their spears into pruning hooks; nation shall not lift up sword against nation, neither shall they learn war any more" (Isaiah 2:4).

There have been relatively few years in our history when somewhere someone has not been waging war on another. Peace is still a much desired and deep-seated need of our world.

(Read Luke 1:68-80.)

Let us pray in silence for peace, as we are directed:

O God, the giver of life and peace, forgive the
    tendency to war, disagreement, and strife which
    we have shown over many years.

Teach us that in the little Child of the manger,
    in his helplessness and promise, lies the way
    to peace, that the way is not in force.

Help us to love all people as we are loved. May
    it be that nation will not rise up against
    nation, nor will power guide our decisions.

Build us up as a loving community of those who,
    as peacemakers, will inherit the earth and be
    called the children of God.

> In Jesus' name we all pray.
>
> Amen.

The Light of Christmas

How dull our celebration of Christmas would be if we did not have the colored lights, the tinsel, and the candles. Our Jewish friends celebrate the Feast of Lights, Hanukkah, at about the same time of the year. In all of the carols, anthems, and songs no one has expressed the place of light any better than Isaiah in chapter 9 (verses 2-7).

The people who walked in the darkness—they have seen a great light. How beautiful it is to enter a darkened chapel and to be handed a long taper as you enter! The only light is on the altar. At the appropriate time the leader and his or her helpers light their candles from the large candle and go through the waiting congregation lighting each taper until the room is aglow with soft, flickering lights.

God sent his only Son into the darkened world to become the Light of the world. No amount of darkness has been able to extinguish that light. Thus, Christmas provides yet another opportunity for you and me to come to share that light. Reach out your slender taper. Allow the warmth and light to guide you. Then go out to share the light with all persons.

Let us pray, in silence, for more light. (Allow time.)

PRAYER

Teach us, O God, the meaning of the light that you send into the world. Help us to transmit that light we have received into the dark places of the earth. Then, all will know that the star shone for them and beckons them to come, worship, and adore.

In Christ we pray.   Amen.

A Service for Advent [1]

PROCESSIONAL: "Prepare the Way for the Lord" [2]

SCENARIO: [3]

1.

In the beginning God created
  the heaven and the earth.
And darkness was upon the face
  of the deep, and the Spirit of God
  moved upon the face of the waters.
And God said, "Let there
  be light." And there was light.
        (See Genesis 1:1-3, KJV.)

In the beginning was the Word,
  and the Word was in the beginning

[1] Program prepared by David Holt and Louise Averill.
[2] From Beryl Red (Nashville: Broadman Press, 1972).
[3] Verses 1 and 2 of the scenario are to be acted out.

with God. All things were made
by him; for in him was life; and
the life was the light of men.
And the light shineth in darkness,
and the darkness comprehendeth it not.
(See John 1:1-5, KJV.)

2.

That was the true Light,
which lighteth every man that
entereth into the world.
That light was in the world,
and the world was made by him,
yet the world knew him not.
(See John 1:9-10, KJV.)

3.

There was a man sent forth from
God. His name was John, which means
"God is gracious." He was sent
to bear witness of the Light
that is the Light of the world.
(See John 1:6-8, KJV.)

And God commanded John:
"Comfort ye, comfort ye my people,
saith your God. Speak comfortingly
to them, that their strife is ended,
that their iniquity is pardoned.
Be the voice of one that crieth in
the wilderness, saying: 'Prepare
ye the way of the Lord.' Every
valley shall be exalted, and every
mountain and hill made low. And the glory
of the Lord shall be revealed." For
the mouth of the Lord hath spoken it.[4]
Prepare ye the way of the Lord.
(See Isaiah 40:1-5, KJV.)

ANTHEM:[5] "Who Is at My Window Who?" by W. Russell

[4] This may be also sung from *Messiah* by Handel.
[5] This anthem is to be sung by the choir and danced creatively by one or two people.

READER: The Lord knocks on your door. Have you listened?

CHOIR: "Hey! Hey! Anybody Listening?"[6]

READER:
> Listen
> Listen! For it is by so doing
> That sound becomes music,
> And noise becomes word.
> Listen! For it is by so doing
> That music becomes inspiration,
> And words grow to be thoughts.
> Listen! For it is by so doing
> That inspiration becomes the joy of action,
> And thoughts of the wise grow to be
> The joy of knowledge.   Listen!

SMALL BAROQUE GROUP OR FULL CHOIR: "Carol of the Advent"[7]

CONGREGATIONAL HYMN: "From Jordan's Bank the Baptist's Cry"

CHORAL READING BY CHOIR OR SMALLER GROUP: Mark 1:2-8

CHOIR ANTHEM: "Ain'-a That Good News"   Spiritual

READER: It is good news that God is sending his only Son into this world. What does it mean to us? Have you heard him knocking? Do you know what it means to become his followers? We have burdens and guilts which deaden our perception. Let us all pray:

PRAYER OF CONFESSION:[8]
> O Lord, who didst create all that is created, who didst make us and fill us with thy breath, giving us free will for good or evil, thou didst send us thyself to be our Light that we might choose thee and shun the darkness.
> Forgive us, for thy law is the law of kindness; forgive our blind eyes, Lord; heal our deaf ears. Open the windows—our eyes—to thy light; open the portals—our ears—and enter.
> Forgive us; redeem us; awaken us now.
>   Amen.

[6] Richard Avery and Donald Marsh, *Hymns Hot and Carols Cool* (Port Jervis, N.Y.: Proclamation Productions, Inc., 1967), p. 5.

[7] Percy Dearmer *et. al., Oxford Book of Carols* (London: Oxford University Press, 1928/1961), pp. 264-265.

[8] This prayer may be chanted freely, and interpretative dance may be used.

VOCAL SOLO: "I Wonder as I Wander" by John Jacob Niles

READER: What wondrous love is this—to accept us just as we are— just as we sit here!

There was a man who complained bitterly that the world was filled with suffering and anguish, neighbor turned against neighbor, and the wounds of humanity too deep ever to be healed. He railed against his friend who believed in listening to his neighbors and sought to love his enemies, saying that no one is *worth* the expense or trouble one takes. His friend replied: "It is better to light a single candle than to curse in the darkness."

CHOIR ANTHEM: "What Wondrous Love Is This"   Shaker tune

SCRIPTURE: Luke 1:5-55

CHOIR ANTHEM: "Let All Mortal Flesh Keep Silence" by Katherine K. Davis

RECESSIONAL: "O Come, O Come, Emmanuel"

4

RESOURCES FOR LENT

Invocation and Offertory Words

First Sunday of Lent: His Face Is Set Toward Jerusalem

Invocation

>Lord, your face is set to go
>to Jerusalem, that great and
>dreaded city of decision.
>As we follow your steps, help us
>to understand the truth—"a servant
>is not greater than his master, nor
>a messenger than the one who sent him."
>Take us deeply into the ways of
>obedience, both counting the cost
>and relying fully upon thy
>great love to sustain us in
>all our ways.

Offertory Word

>You have chosen us, O Master,
>to be your faithful followers.
>Even when we falter and fall short

of your great love,
Help us to know that you will
never leave us nor forsake us.

Second Sunday in Lent: The Baptism

Invocation

Lord,
Baptized to fulfill the law;
Call, Lord,
Our hearts to thy throne in awe;
Bring us, Lord,
To the river of thy love;
Baptize us, Lord,
With the fire and the dove.

Offertory Word

Prepare us, Lord,
For thy gentle mercy's sake
That we, Lord,
May return the love we take.

Third Sunday in Lent: True Greatness

"'But you must not be called "rabbi"; for you have one Rabbi, and you are all brothers. Do not call any man on earth "father"; for you have one Father, and he is in heaven. . . . The greatest among you must be your servant. For whoever exalts himself will be humbled; and whoever humbles himself will be exalted'" (Matthew 23:8-12, NEB).

Invocation

Hearken unto our yearnings, O Lord,
for we need your presence.
Help us to know the meaning of
true greatness found in thee
and in following your way.
The ways of the world are ever with us;
may they never be our guide.
Wean us from earth, move through our
beings, and have your perfect way
in our obedient hearts.

Offertory Word

> All that we have and own we
>   have received from your hand.
> In deep gratitude, O God, we
>   now give of ourselves to you.
> May the self-giving of thy Son
>   constantly strengthen us to a
>   greatness not of ourselves.
> Accept our gifts in his name
>   we pray.

> Amen.

Fourth Sunday in Lent: The Miracles

". . . to heal the brokenhearted, to preach deliverance to the captives, and recovering of sight to the blind . . ." (Luke 4:18, KJV).

Invocation

> Hearken unto our cry, Lord Jesus;
> We need thy healing.
> Our minds—twisting, lamed, and limited—
> Need the healing of thy wisdom and grace.
>
> Our spirits are blind to thy presence;
> Let thy light fill us.
> Through dark doubts and shadowed sorrows, Lord,
> Work thy miracles to lighten our hearts.

Offertory Word

> Release us from the captivity
> Of our lonely thoughts;
> Bind us now with thy demanding love
> That we may freely give ourselves to thee.

The Fifth Sunday in Lent: The Teachings

Invocation

> The hillsides of Galilee
> Echoed with thy words, O Lord—
> Teach us now that we may live.
> The hill of Gethsemane
> Trembled at thy prayer's power—
> Teach us to prepare for death.

The dark hill of Calvary
Shook our wild world around—
Teach us, Lord, that we may give.

Offertory Word

On a hill alone with thee,
Holding thy power in our hands—
Teach us to love for eternity.

Sixth Sunday in Lent: The Triumphal Entry

"Remember where you stand: not before the palpable, blazing fire of Sinai, with the darkness, gloom, and whirlwind, the trumpet-blast and the oracular voice. . . .

"No, you stand before Mount Zion and the city of the living God, heavenly Jerusalem. . . . See that you do not refuse to hear the voice that speaks. Those who refused to hear the oracle speaking on earth found no escape; still less shall we escape if we refuse to hear the One who speaks from heaven" (Hebrews 12:18-25, NEB).

Invocation

Today, our Father, we will hear
the shouts of praise to Jesus
as he rides into the city.
The coats will be strewed in the
way, and the palms will be waved.
Hosanna! Hosanna to the One who comes
in the name of the Lord!
As we join in the procession,
keep our hearts tender to the
betrayals and costs of discipleship.
May thy great love sustain us now
and in the days before us.

Offertory Word

We would bless him who comes in
the name of the Lord.
We come out to meet you with
our gifts of mind and heart.
May these our offerings be the
tokens that we lay our lives
on your altar this day and
in all the days of our living.

Easter Morning

Invocation

> If we did not rejoice on this day,
> Then the very stone
> Which rolled away from the light-filled tomo
> Would call out that the Lord is risen.
>
> If we did not praise the living Christ,
> Then the morning sun
> Which saw him stand upon the third day
> Would thunder, "The Redeemer liveth!"

Offertory Word

> Behind us, death is a broken stone;
> Christ is our bright sunrise,
> And alone in the garden we hear
> His voice call our names.

Palm Sunday Prayer

Today is Palm Sunday. We reflect once more, our Father, that it was on that first Palm Sunday that your Son received such acclamation on the road into Jerusalem. As the palm branches were tossed in the roadway, the people shouted, "Hosanna! Hosanna!"

We rejoice again this day that the King, our Lord Jesus Christ, is coming to be ruler of our hearts. May we prepare for his coming in the full knowledge of what will happen in the week of the Passion.

We give heartfelt thanks that your love to your children has not changed, that you desire each of us to respond in love and devotion, that your salvation awaits all who will accept.

May this happy day be the first of many when we say from the heart, "Hosanna! Hosanna! Blessed is he who comes in the name of the Lord."

A Litany of the Cross

LEADER: O God, in whose grace and glory we have our lives, we come to acknowledge our debt to you. In your self-giving for our salvation you have demonstrated again and again that you love us.

RESPONSE: O Lord, make us thankful.

LEADER: For all who have given their lives in service, sacrifice, and even death, in their devotion to the gospel,

RESPONSE: O Lord, make us thankful.

LEADER: For the cross of your Son, for the dark days leading up to the cross, and for his love so freely given to us and all persons,

RESPONSE: O Lord, make us thankful.

LEADER: For the Lenten season when we can recount the loneliness of the Garden, the suffering, shame, and rejection which our Lord endured, for his unfailing faith in you and all humankind,

RESPONSE: O Lord, make us thankful.

LEADER: Teach us that except we walk through the darkness, we cannot appreciate the light; that except we see the cross clearly, we will not understand the empty tomb; that except we obey even to the point of sacrifice, we cannot truly be your disciples.
          In the name of Christ Jesus we pray.   Amen.

Meditations for Holy Week

Monday—Cleansing the Temple

Suggested Scriptures: Jeremiah 7:1-15
                      Luke 19:41-48

When our blessed Lord looked out across Jerusalem, he wept. Jerusalem was unmoved by the word of the Lord that had come to it; the city was unrepentant and unresponding. The people "did not recognize God's moment when it came."

So Jesus went to the heart of the nation's business and drove out the money changers from the temple. The game was up, the opposition gelled, and Jesus was to be destroyed.

PRAYER:

Our first words to you, O God, should be those of contrition and confession. Like the dwellers in Jerusalem we, too, have been unmindful of your coming and your desire to reign over us. Grant us your forgiveness we pray.

Then, O Father, we would accept your love and your self-giving in Jesus of Nazareth. As we see his deeds, listen to his words, respond to his call to discipleship, may we never forget your care for your children.

May we never be careless or take you for granted. In the name of your Son, we pray.   Amen.

BENEDICTION:

Go forth into the world in the confidence that God loves you and has sent his Son into that same world to redeem you. Turn not your back upon him, but in all diligence follow his truth now and always.

Amen.

Tuesday—The Stone Rejected

Suggested Scriptures: Isaiah 5:1-7
Luke 20:9-20

Jesus told a parable to those in the temple who had demanded of him some authority for his teaching. It was the parable of the vineyard owner who left his vineyard in the care of servants. When he sent to receive an accounting of the property, the servants killed those sent and refused to be responsible for their actions. Finally the owner sent his son to receive an accounting. They killed him, too, in the hope that the owner would give up and the property would become theirs.

Jesus then quoted to them the Scripture—"The stone which the builders rejected has become the main corner-stone."

Many times rejected and despitefully used, Jesus has become the Christ, the Lord and Savior of all who will follow him and give him their allegiance. Once more the strange ways of God prove to be more enduring than the ways of humankind. The stone is set at the center, and we build upon it.

PRAYER:

We pause, our Father, on this Tuesday of Holy Week to respond to your love. Help us to recognize the stone which is to become our cornerstone and not to be blinded to your revealing. Take us like clay in the hands of a potter and make us into vessels fit for your use. Fill us with your Spirit, then send us out into the world to share the Good News with all others.

In the name of your Son we pray.   Amen.

BENEDICTION:

May the God who enters the temples of our hearts in the person of his Son go with us now and remain with us so we may become his obedient children now and evermore.   Amen.

Wednesday—The Temple Replaced

Suggested Scriptures: Jeremiah 22:1-9
Luke 21:1-19

As a part of his general challenge to Jerusalem, Jesus had a conversation with some folk who were admiring its beauty and grandeur. He told them to beware of putting their trust in material things, even things that seemed as central and enduring as the temple. Jesus spoke of ominous days ahead. There would be persecution and hardship; the city would be sacked and the temple destroyed.

People always find it hard to envision a new day when all will be destroyed and when everything we've valued is returned to dust. The saving phrase in all of the twenty-first chapter of Luke is found in verse 19. "By standing firm you will win true life for yourselves" (NEB).

No city, no temple, no church, no edifice no matter how beautiful or enduring can be the heart of our faith. Our salvation is centered in the God who is worshiped in these temples; but even though the temple fall, "the Word of the Lord abides forever."

PRAYER:

Forgive us, our Father, for those times when we have worshiped temples or idols or any self-made image rather than you. Set our minds and hearts upon your eternal truths that never perish. May all our buildings and all our creations be the means through which your gospel is heard and your name proclaimed through all the earth.

In the name of your Son we pray.   Amen.

BENEDICTION:

Go with God and God go with you. Serve him with all your mind, heart, soul, and spirit; and love your neighbor as yourself. Amen.

Thursday—The Covenant Renewed

Suggested Scriptures: Exodus 12:21-28
                                    Luke 22:1-23

The Passover, or the Feast of Unleavened Bread, as it was called, was a day of deep remembering for the people of Israel. It commemorated deliverance from foreign domination and slavery; it reminded Israel of the need for obedience. It was a solemn occasion.

How fitting then, that as the final days of conflict approached, Jesus took the Twelve and went to a borrowed upper room to celebrate the feast. To this very day Christians all over the world celebrate this feast calling it by various names: the Eucharist, the Last Supper, the Communion.

There Jesus took the bread and the wine. As he distributed them to the disciples, he associated the bread with his body about to be broken and the wine with his blood about to be spilled.

Things visible become for us symbols of things unseen, the self-giving and love of God in his Son for you and for me.

PRAYER:

Whenever we come to the table of the Lord and take into our hands bread and wine, may we be conscious of the costliness of these emblems. May our memories be awakened to recall the rock from which we were hewed. May our spirits be quickened to a renewed obedience. Feed us with the bread and wine that we hunger and thirst only after righteousness.

In the name of your Son we pray. Amen.

BENEDICTION:

We go forth from the upper room to the duties of every day. May the memory of Christ's love sustain us and enable us to share the living bread with all we meet. Amen.

Friday—The Crucifixion

Suggested Scriptures: Genesis 22:1-18
Luke 22:63–23:49

Sometimes we need to be reminded that Jesus was not crucified on a gold cross carefully centered between golden candlesticks but on a rude gibbet stuck up on a garbage heap outside a city.

The cross, symbol of defeat and death, is the final act of the self-giving God who withheld nothing of himself, not even his dearly beloved Son. The cross was the darkest point of human history, the seeming end of all that Jesus had preached and taught, the seeming triumph of evil over good.

We need to descend to the deepest agonies of the cross in order to understand truly the glories of Easter Day. One could not have had its meaning without the other. So it is that the hymn writer reminds us:

> There was no other good enough
> To pay the price of sin;
> He only could unlock the gate
> Of heaven, and let us in.

All roads in human history start at the cross of Christ.

PRAYER:

We cannot understand your great love, O God, but we accept it and thank you for it. We rejoice that the cross could not be the end, that death was not able to defeat your life. Help us to understand the agony of death that we may the better participate in his life.

In the name of your Son we pray. Amen.

BENEDICTION:

Beneath the cross of Jesus, we fain would take our stand. May its shadow always remind us that we are bought with a terrible price. May we always live in the life our Lord Jesus Christ came to bring.

Amen.

5

PERSONAL AND INTERPERSONAL WORSHIP

Private Prayers

As with public prayers, even more with private prayers is there the danger of the humdrum and the repetitious. For this reason many people find the use of devotional booklets with a Scripture, thought, and prayer for each day to be useful. But even here, they can be read and remain somewhat distant from us.

We are suggesting the following few prayers in the hope that you will sit down with paper and pen and write some of your own prayers. Even if you do not use them in your private devotional periods, they will have value for stimulating new forms of expression in your prayers. Prayer is as much an attitude as a form of expression, and our attitude to God can be enhanced by more careful attention to our prayer life.

At the Beginning of the Day

Open our hearts, O Father, to the light of this your new day. May the warmth of the sun gladden our home, and may the light of your presence keep us close to you and one another.

Keep us from sin and selfishness, and make our journey this day one which will bring us nearer you.

In the name of Christ we pray.   Amen.

At a Time of Change

We go out into the world, our Father, with uncertainty, fear, and a spirit of timidity in our hearts. We know there will be changes that affect our whole being and disturb the serenity we have come to depend upon.

As we put our hand in yours, go with us and help us to face each change we experience in our lives in the confidence of your presence and your power.

Through Christ Jesus we pray.   Amen.

For Families

O God, in your wisdom you have put us in families and you have been pleased to bless us with your presence. Forgive us those times when we have not honored your presence, when we have been selfish, mean, and inconsiderate with one another. Help us to cherish all the good experiences and continue to share them in our homes and with all those whom we meet day by day. So may our homes be places of love and grace where you are ever present.

Through Christ we pray.   Amen.

In Times of Loss

O God, do draw near to us in this time of separation and loneliness. We confess our failure of nerve and faith. The times we need to be strong, we are weak; the times we need most to believe, we become doubting.

You know all about us, and we realize you will not leave us or fail to forgive us as we confess our failures. Draw near to us; we pray that your strength may fill us and enable us to face even this loss to your greater glory.

Through our blessed Lord we pray.   Amen.

For the Gifts of Life

All around us are signs of your gracious bounty, O God, our Lord. Your gifts to us are so many we can hardly list them before you. Keep us from taking any of them for granted or thinking that we are totally deserving of them. May we count our blessings and remember always that it is your nature to give and not count the cost.

Fill us with gratitude, we pray, in the name of Jesus our Savior, your greatest gift to us.   Amen.

Family Prayers

Our Father, you have been pleased to put us in families, and you have blessed us in myriad ways. We know you would control our lives and bless them with your power if we would allow you total sway in us. Teach us to return your love and care so we may become more loving and caring for one another. May this be the place where we are loved in spite of all our sins and shortcomings.

Through Jesus Christ we pray.   Amen.

We rejoice, our Father, in the knowledge that our Lord lived with his family in Nazareth and shared its joys and hardships. As we reflect on our life together, we would confess that it has been far from perfect. We have been mean, nasty, short-tempered, and cruel. But we have also loved, cared, served, and supported one another, and we have known your love in our lives. May we ever be open to your guidance that we "may grow in wisdom, stature, and favor with God and man" (see Luke 2:52).   Amen.

Like the apostle Paul, we so often find ourselves doing those things we ought not to do and leaving undone those things we ought to do. We confess our sins of commission and omission. Help us to encourage one another in our homes, to support one another with kindly comment, to seek for what is best in your sight for all of the family. May we drop all sham and pretense and be the best we can to your glory and honor.

Through Christ we ask it.   Amen.

We would ask you, O God, that our homes may become such centers of your love that all who enter may be at home with us and you. So transform our life-style that we may feel free to invite others to come and sit at our table and share the warmth of our fellowship.

We know this can come only because of your grace and power, and we dedicate ourselves to that in Jesus' name.   Amen.

Our Father in Heaven, come again into our homes and dwell with us. We recognize our need of your help if we are to be the faithful followers of the Christ we would hope to be. Where we have sinned, do forgive us, we pray; where we have failed to hear your voice, sharpen our awareness; for our times of doubt, increase our faith; support all our good efforts with your strength and blessing, and make us ever more amenable to your love.

Hear us, in the name of our blessed Lord, we pray.　　Amen.

Table Graces

Grant, O God, that these gifts of your bounty
May strengthen us in mind and body
The better to serve you.　　Amen.

For these and all your mercies
So graciously provided for us, O God,
We give you our thanks.　　Amen.

May we be content, our God, with just a little less
So others in the world may have a little more.　　Amen.

Grace our table with your presence, O God.
As we partake of these good gifts so graciously prepared,
May we be strengthened for your service.　　Amen.

Be present at our table, Lord.
Be here and everywhere adored.
These mercies bless, and grant that we
May nourished for your service be.　　Amen.

For food and friends
And all God's gifts, we give you praise.　　Amen.

O the Lord is good to me,
　and so I thank the Lord
For giving me the things I need—

The sun and the rain and the apple seed.
O the Lord is good to me.   (Johnny Appleseed)

O God, for the things we ask of you,
May we also be willing to work.   Amen.

Prayers While Visiting

Members of the Christian church visit one another and friends who are not connected with the church, under many different circumstances. In many of these visits it would seem appropriate to share together in the fellowship of prayer. Some of these occasions are, of course, sickness, bereavement, birth, marriage, loss, promotion, honor, etc.

However, our experience has been that people find these moments to be extremely painful because they just don't seem to know what to say or how to say it. This is a classic example of where we have left the praying to the preacher, and even some of them experience difficulty under these circumstances.

It might not be inappropriate at this point to mention that you are a guest in the home where you are visiting. Take due care to determine that the residents of the home are able to respond to the suggestion that you offer prayer. However, don't use the uncertainty of the moment as a cover for your own unwillingness. If you can develop this gift as a natural and meaningful part of your fellowship in the gospel, you will find it to be warmly received and deeply appreciated by those in unusual circumstances.

General

Our Father, we rejoice in one another's presence and in yours. We know that you are never far from any of us and that your help is always available. Teach us the meaning of a life lived in your presence. Help us to be aware that in the world of nature, in our conversation with one another, in our work and play you can speak to us.

May our lives be enriched and strengthened and our purpose to be your obedient children, clarified; through Christ we pray.   Amen.

Sorrow

Our hearts are heavy, O God, as we stand together in the midst of loss. You have promised never to leave us nor forsake us; so we come claiming your promise. Draw especially near to these your children in their need. Walk beside them in the way. Help them to rely upon your strength and to know that in the long pull your will may be made known to them. Surround us with your love, and help us to know your love never fails.

In the name of Jesus our Lord, we pray.   Amen.

Sickness

Our friend is ill, O God, as you know. We come together today asking that if it be your will she [he] will experience healing and restoration of health and strength. Above all, however, we would ask of you that your presence may be with our loved ones in all of these crises. Give wisdom and understanding to those whose responsibility it is to look after the sick; grant patience to all of us who wait.

Grant, we beseech you, a special share of your grace according to your love as revealed in Jesus Christ in whose name we pray.

Amen.

Visitation on Behalf of the Church

We bring you grateful thanks, O God, that you have called us unto yourself and made us part of the Body of Christ. Many times we have failed in our attempts to be your representatives in the world, and we ask your forgiveness for our failures.

Help us to become open to your love being revealed in all of life. Teach us how to share that love in our homes and in the congregation of the faithful in the world. So may it be that your will may be known on earth even as it is known in heaven.

Hear us in the name of him who taught us when we pray to say: "Our Father, who art in heaven. . . ."

Outdoor, Camping Worship

Many years ago the psalmist declared, "The heavens declare the glory of God; and the firmament sheweth his handywork" (Psalm 19:1, KJV). Ever since, men and women have found some of their most precious worship moments in the outdoors. As we have increased time for leisure, we have more time for reflection and observation.

The camping movement has burgeoned to such an extent that literally millions of people on the North American continent are heading for the wide open spaces as families and other groups. We would like to suggest a few of the resources which you can use to aid your own worship of God in the outdoors and which you can share with others. We have focused our worship around the following: the camp fire, the quietness of an isolated place, the stars and the heavens, the waves of lake and sea.

The Camp Fire

At day's end it is good to sit with friends and watch the play of the fire as it dances a message of warmth and light. Fire reminds us of a lot of good things. We respect its power, but the warmth and the glow remind us of the many good experiences we have had in our Christian fellowship. A fire seems to draw us together and make all of the world out there seem far away, at least for those few moments.

PRAYER: Thank you, O God, for this fire. For the warmth and love that you have given to us here and in many of our experiences, for these quiet moments of rest from the busyness of life, we bless you. May we be truly conscious that you are always near us, and may we ever seek to share the warmth of our love with all we meet.

In Jesus' name we pray. Amen.

Quietness

It isn't until we get far away from village or city that we realize how much noise and din surrounds us. There in the quiet seclusion of the outdoors we feast on the silence. Silence bothers some people; it is a strange feeling not to hear a radio, a TV, or at least background noise. But here, we can share with others a deep respect for the meditative possibilities, for quietness and peace that surround us.

PRAYER: With the psalmist we would come to you, our Father, in quietness and confidence. As we listen to the crackling of branches, the distant call of a late returning bird, the lap of water on the shore, help us to drink deeply of the peace, the tranquility of your world. Give peace to the hurried, and in our silences may we hear your still small voice. Amen.

The Stars and the Heavens

It is only as we move away from the bright lights of the main street that we begin to see the stars. Too numerous to count, like the sand on the beach, they stretch endlessly on beyond our sight. "The heavens declare the glory of God; and the firmament sheweth his handywork" (Psalm 19:1, KJV). For centuries persons have used the stars to guide their travels. May we now pause and allow them to restore to us perspective, a true sense of the universe of which we are a part.

PRAYER: Teach us, O Creator God, in the midst of your vast universe that we are your children. Give us a deepened understanding of your creation that we may stand in awe and truly worship you. Help us to take as good care of our part of the universe as we can. May we not waste or despoil, and may all your creatures live in harmony with one another and with their world.

In Christ's name we pray.   Amen.

The Waves of the Lake

As waves break upon the shore following one another in seemingly endless procession, our minds turn to the power of our world. People have always had thoughts of harnessing that power but in most times have had to content themselves with protecting the shorelines from erosion.

As we look at the restlessness of the waves, as we hear the constant sounds of the breaking waves, let us meditate on the power of God, equally endless; and let us be aware of our relationship to that power.

PRAYER: In the same way as the power of the water breaks over the shore, O God, may we see your power in our lives. Teach us afresh, we pray you, of the greatness of our world. Help us as we meditate upon the grandeur and the majesty of creation to understand that we are part of that creation, that you have made us for fellowship with yourself. May your love, as limitless as the sea, come into our lives.

In the name of Jesus Christ we pray.   Amen.

A New Year's Litany

LEADER: O God, who has been from eternity, at the beginning of this new year we pause in your presence, and

RESPONSE: We lift up our hearts to you, O Lord.

LEADER: We recognize that the past year has been filled with failures and sins, that we have not always been responsive to your will; in the recognition of our failures,

RESPONSE: We lift up our hearts to you, O Lord.

LEADER: Give us fresh courage to accept your forgiveness and renewed strength for this year. Aid us in every good effort whenever we do your will and serve your greater purposes; for your power

RESPONSE: We lift up our hearts to you, O Lord.

LEADER: Keep us from loss of faith or despair that evil so often seems to triumph over good. Help us to know that we are called to be faithful and not successful, keep us from substituting our agendas for yours and help us always to

RESPONSE: Lift up our hearts to you, O Lord.

6

SOURCES OF IDEAS FOR WORSHIP

One of the most frequent questions of all persons in every generation is, "How can we pray, and what ought our prayers be about?" The prayer of our blessed Lord which we call the Lord's Prayer was prefaced by such questioning. And he answered, "When you pray, say. . . ."

Our basic contention is that many of our prayers and meditation ideas come directly from our involvement in and observation of the world around us. As we are engaged in conversation, in reading, in the changes of the seasons, in triumphs, and in the tragedies of life around us, all of these give content to our prayers.

To be a leader in worship is to assume a most important task. It is not one to be taken lightly. No matter how little you have to do in a particular service, take it very sincerely and be prepared to do it to the best of your abilities. Careful attention to the theme or the course of the service will provide focus and prevent a diffusion of concentration that weakens or diverts the attention of your worshiping group.

We have included a wide variety of thought starters in these next pages. They range all the way from the very traditional to the novel. In a few instances we have included some humorous episodes. These discoveries have come out of the shared experience of people seeking to express their joys, sorrows, love, praise, hopes, and aspirations to almighty God in worship. We would encourage you to become more observant, more innovative, and more venturesome in worship. Dr. R. J. McCracken, one of our teachers, used to say, "God loves a hilarious giver." This is an image that we carry with real meaning and true pleasure. It is our earnest prayer that God may guide us in a more satisfying means of communing with him and with his children with whom we worship.

Some Observations

You will notice that the prayers and meditations in most of the sections of this book are usable with some modification in other settings. You will note, also, that the prayers (brief) take up the concerns expressed in the presentations. Worship, even when as brief as these examples suggest, does have to have continuity. You should be able to sum up in your prayer the main concern raised in the worship period.

It is important to be able to deal with one thought in a devotion within a meeting. If you get too profound or involved in your presentation, God will understand, but those who are a part of the worship will not, and they need to know that they are partners in expressing concerns to God. The thought must be sensible and well worked out but ought not to be complicated. If you feel the need to express something in depth, the worship period in such a meeting is not the time or place. The worshiper ought to avoid any tendency to use the period of worship to deliver a lecture.

Quotes That Provoke

All around us are words, symbols, stories, and experiences that help us center on our relationship to God and others. In this section we invite you to listen more perceptively to the words of others that they may lead you to praise God more effectively.

The following "quotes" come from two posters, the Bible (our greatest source of affirmatives and faith), another book, and the cover of a newsletter. Every day you will encounter similar provocative sayings which you will want to share with others. In each of these selections we have paralleled words from Scripture, and we suggest that you may wish to do the same with the quotes you find.

Look around you; stop and listen. You will be provoked to worship.

Quotes from a Poster

Time is too slow
for those who wait;
Too swift
for those who fear;
Too long
for those who grieve;
Too short
for those who rejoice.
But for those who love,
time is not.

Time, like a lot of other things in our lives, is relative to our state of mind at the moment. It is not controllable but at times seems to crawl; at other times, fairly to fly. Time is one of the most precious gifts we have; each of us is given exactly twenty-four hours each day of our lives.

So the important thing is: What do we do with the time that is ours?

Read Ecclesiastes 3:1-8. Use these verses to be reminded of the use we make of our time, and let us ask God to make us worthy recipients of our lives and our opportunities.

Martin Buber has said that all real living is meeting.[1] The Bible is full of incidents where people met and were met. God met Adam in the Garden of Eden; Abraham met God high on the mountain, and his son Isaac was delivered back to Abraham when he had resolved to make of him a sacrifice; some unknown visitors came to Mamre and told Abraham and Sarah she was to bear a child; the psalmist met his Shepherd in the deeps of a gloomy valley; the disciples met their Master on the lakeshore; and the apostle Paul met his Lord on the roadway.

Meetings are times of potential, times to be open to new experiences, new hopes, new life. We do not know what Isaiah expected when he went into the temple, but what he did meet there changed his entire life.

(Read Isaiah 6:1-10.)

PRAYER:

O God, in the midst of our all-too-busy lives we would meet you

[1] Martin Buber, *Between Man and Man* (Boston: Beacon Press, 1955).

and those who are yours. Keep us open and available that every encounter may provide a fresh opportunity of fellowship with you. Open our eyes and our ears that we may truly see and hear.

In your name we pray.   Amen.

From the Cover of a Newsletter

"An artist enters eagerly into the life of man, of all men.
    He becomes all men in himself.
The function of the artist is to disturb.
His duty is to arouse the sleeper,
    to shake the complacent pillars of the world.
He reminds the world of its dark ancestry,
Shows the world its present, and points the way to its
    new birth.
He makes uneasy the static, the set, and the still."

Paul Tillich is reported to have said: "Sometimes I think my mission is to bring faith to the faithless and doubt to the faithful."

These quotations underline the often forgotten dilemma of the Christian. We do march to the beat of a strange drum, and we do take our directions for life from an "other-worldly" source. Sometimes we need to affirm that which is good and thank God that he works in mysterious ways. Sometimes we need to be critical of supposedly good things we cannot in good conscience accept or support.

(Read Isaiah 55, especially verses 6-8.)

PRAYER:

Grant us the serenity to accept the things we cannot change, the courage to change the things we can, and the wisdom to know the difference.   Amen.

Our Stake in the Church

"The Church is old in the sense that it is the continuation of the life of Israel, the People of God. It is new in the sense that it is founded on the revelation made through Jesus Christ of God's final purpose for mankind."[2]

We all tend to be greatly comforted by the heritage out of which we have come, and we are also grateful that the old, old stories have relevance and deep meaning for us today. Jesus tells an interesting story of the wise man who reaches into his tradition for the old yet has at his fingertips the new.

[2] R.N. Flew, *Jesus and His Church* (London: Epworth Press, 1938), p. 135.

(Read Matthew 13:44-52.)

"The kingdom of heaven is like treasure hidden in a field . . . is like a net which was thrown into the sea." These old parables help us to reflect on the life of Christ in our midst. They are old but have direct application for every life with which they come in contact. Perhaps we can recapture a sense of the permanency of our foundations and on that base relate in a new way to God, to other believers, and to the world for which Christ died.

PRAYER:

Help us, our loving Father, to let the eternal truths of your gospel come into our lives so we may illumine the present and make your will known on earth as it is already known in heaven.   Amen.

Thoughts for Good Living

If a child lives with criticism,
    he learns to condemn.
If a child lives with hostility,
    he learns to fight.
If a child lives with fear,
    he learns to be apprehensive.
If a child lives with jealousy,
    he learns to feel guilty.
If a child lives with tolerance,
    he learns to be patient.
If a child lives with encouragement,
    he learns to be confident.
If a child lives with praise,
    he learns to be appreciative.
If a child lives with acceptance,
    he learns to love.
If a child lives with approval,
    he learns to like himself.
If a child lives with recognition,
    he learns it is good to have a goal.
If a child lives with honesty,
    he learns what the truth is.
If a child lives with fairness,
    he learns to have faith in himself
    and those about him.
If a child lives with friendliness,
    he learns that the world is a nice place in which to live.[3]

[3] From "The Highlander" (the monthly publication of the Rotary Club of Dundas, Ontario), 1970.

From the Bible

(Read John 6:32-40 from *The Jerusalem Bible*)

What is it that sustains our families, our children, and those especially dependent upon us? The symbol of Jesus as the bread, the most basic of food for the body and the spirit, is an arresting idea. As we offer ourselves to God in humble service, seeking to embody that bread, let us realize that it is not our strength but our obedience that counts. The good gifts are God's, as is the power; we are but vehicles, freely and wholly committed, hopefully, to God's use.

In the Beginning

Everyone is looking for a starting place. Where will we begin? Let's go back to "square one."

Genesis 1:1-12 describes the first three days of creation. It starts with the tremendous faith statement "In the beginning God. . . ." When we go over to the New Testament writer John, we see how he has taken a page out of the Genesis writer's book. John 1:1-14 begins, "In the beginning was the Word. . . ."

The rooting of all of our existence in the self-giving of God gives us a sense of due humility and also of firm confidence that we are part of the divine creation and we have been called to share in that life.

We may not be able to go back to the beginning, but we can join the psalmist in giving thanks to the Creator God for the lovely world he created and for allowing us to share in it.

Psalm 19 says: "The heavens declare the glory of God . . ." (KJV).

Bumper Stickers That Say More

Really, ideas are everywhere. Most bumper stickers tend to be related to local issues, such as pollution control, conservation, boycotts, strikes, etc. Some, of course, are in poor taste and are best forgotten. Many, however, as we have tried to suggest with the following four, help us to center on some essential truths and, perchance, to worship.

Nor should we be too sober in all of our approaches to worship. I saw an amusing bumper sticker in Adelaide, Australia, on a car of ancient vintage: "In case of the rapture, this vehicle will be unoccupied." Another said quite simply, "Ban bumper stickers." We feel certain that the God who created the camel, the donkey, ducks, and drakes wishes us to enjoy life and offer our enjoyments to him in worship.

◄—Pass Side——Suicide —►

In most of life's endeavors there's an acceptable way of doing things and there's an unacceptable way. This is particularly true on a busy highway. It is much safer to overtake another driver in an expected and approved manner than to surprise him or her by innovation. The bumper sticker exaggerates, but it gets its message across.

There are many opportunities which come to us each day that allow us to help people find the "pass side" of their lives. Jesus spoke of the necessity to share the cup of cold water with the thirsty and the crust of bread with those who hunger (Matthew 25:35). We need to be aware of those times when we can share the bounty we enjoy in our lives.

The simplest of all acts we can perform is that of listening to someone. We may be the first one to have really listened, and the results could be dramatic.

PRAYER:

We have bread, water, and time, O God. Help us to use these simple but profound gifts of yours to the good of all and particularly those we meet every day.

To your honor and glory we ask this.   Amen.

Don't Follow Me. I'm Lost.

The humor of a bumper sticker with such a message brightens even a dark day. And, as often happens, it says a lot more than what is printed. Many people, not all of them in automobiles, are looking for a leader, someone to follow, someone who knows the way even in the dark.

Jesus had a conversation with some unbelieving Jews on one occasion. He had been speaking of his Father and spoke of himself as a light to be followed. The Jews asked for more direction. The reply was, "I am going away. You will look for me, but you will die in your sin; where I am going you cannot come" (John 8:21, NEB).

(Read John, chapter 8.)

Jesus promises in verses 31-32 that if these hearers will make his word their own and will be his disciples, they will learn the truth; and that truth will make them free.

PRAYER:

We live in a world where almost everyone is giving us directions, O

God. Help us to discern your voice among the noisy crowds, and help us to obey that voice which alone will lead us to the truth which will make us free.

In Jesus' name we pray.   Amen.

Have a Nice Day

What a benediction it is to come up behind a car on a crowded freeway, feeling frustrated, and suddenly there it is—*Have a Nice Day!* It's a considerate message of good will that breathes fresh air into our polluted environment and helps us to smile just a little more. How like the words of Jesus as recorded in John 14:1, "Let not your hearts be troubled," or, in *The Jerusalem Bible,* "Do not let your hearts be troubled." Jesus' followers are deeply disturbed at the prospects of his betrayal and of his instant departure from them. Peter has just been told that he will deny his Lord. The words of Jesus are designed to strengthen their faith. The entire fourteenth chapter spells out the details of what God is prepared to do for them and why they should not fear when he is the way, the truth, and the life for them.

PRAYER:

Forgive us, our Father, that we become discouraged and fearful when the pressures of life push in upon us. Keep us from ever thinking that we are dependent upon our own strength. Make us more willing to avail ourselves of your power and presence so that we really need never be troubled.

In Jesus' name we pray.   Amen.

Don't Blame Me, I Voted. . . .

Nobody wants to take the blame for the mess our world is in. If one party is in power, people will claim to have voted for the opposite party. One is tempted to wonder who really did vote for those in power and how they got elected. However, the refusal to be responsible is a tendency of which we need to be aware and over which we need to ponder. We, those of us who name the name of Christ, are responsible. We are called by his name, and we represent him just as surely and just as directly as we represent ourselves.

Jesus speaks these beautiful words:

> You did not choose me,
> no, I chose you;

and I commissioned you
to go out and bear fruit,
fruit that will last;
and then the Father will give you
anything you ask him in my name.
What I command you
is to love one another.
John 15:16-17 *(The Jerusalem Bible)*

So we can no longer say, "Don't blame me." And if we are going to accept responsibility, it behooves us to avail ourselves of the power of God so that we can love and be responsible.

PRAYER:

You have loved us, O God, and commanded us to love. Help us to share your love with all we meet in your name and for your sake.

Amen.

Worship Through Paintings

Sometimes our thoughts of God defy expression, and no matter how hard we try to verbalize them, they still won't come. At times like these, persons have taken to the arts as mediums of expression. Doubtless you have your favorite pieces of art which immediately suggest themselves as ways of worship.

We have suggested two quite different ones. The more traditional painting of Dürer has been reproduced in wood, two prints, and in plaster. The directness and simplicity of the painting speaks to everyone. The selection of Salvador Dali is a most successful attempt to break through our traditional point of view and our perspective to look more intensively at the figure on the cross.

We hope that these may be sufficiently provocative for you to build on them using your favorite art pieces.

Praying Hands

Secure a print of the painting and place it in a prominent place for all to see. It is clearly a picture that quickly conveys its message to each beholder in simple, lovely directness.

It is interesting, however, to hear the popular interpretation that is often given of how Albrecht Dürer came to paint this picture. He had grown up in poverty. Most of his attempts to earn a living and

PRAYING HANDS
Albrecht Durer

CHRIST OF ST. JOHN OF THE CROSS
Salvador Dali

continue to paint ended in frustration. The other artist with whom he lived was equally torn between the necessity of working and his preference for painting.

They resolved the issue by the friend going to work full-time to release Dürer to paint. One day Dürer discovered his friend at prayer and resolved to paint those hands as his recognition of what they had meant to him and as an inspiration for all who would see them in future years. The hands of toil lifted in prayer tie the life of labor and of contemplation together.

Perhaps even now, they will help us to give grateful thanks to God for work and for prayer and for the relationship between the two.

Christ of St. John of the Cross

Secure a print of this arresting picture by Salvador Dali, and set it before your group so everyone can see it clearly and reflect on its meaning.

What a strangely moving picture it is. The whole point of view commands the viewer's immediate attention and causes questions to flow. It is a picture that seems to reflect the available light around it; as the shadows of the day change, so do the moods which are projected by the painting change.

Your attention is riveted on the Christ figure; the drawn muscles of arms and shoulders telegraph tension. The light source illumines the figure on the cross but the background remains dark, ominous. Then your eye moves to the world below, for this cross is suspended high above those wondering fishermen as they stand beside their boat and nets. They haven't looked up; are they aware that a Man hangs on that cross? Is it possible that that particular death can be of no consequence to them?

And suppose that cross were suspended over our community in the here and now. Could we walk about at our predetermined tasks as though nothing had happened? We could. And some do. The Bible reminds us from the beginning that the idea of the cross is a troublesome one. Read 1 Corinthians 1:17-25. The language of the cross may be illogical for some; others see it as God's power to save.

7

AIDS TO WORSHIP

In the past, the Christian church used symbols, such as art, music, architecture, and fabric to set the atmosphere for worship. Some aspects of the Reformation removed much of this part of worship in fear that the art forms were either being worshiped for themselves or were being used as crutches. The contention was that people should be able to worship a God they love without aids, that worship should come from the heart. Time has shown that with care the beauty and communication of symbols can be just as effective in aiding worship as the spoken word. In the present day, nearly all churches are returning to these forms of worship aids to add variety and depth to the worship experience. Probably in these more than in any other area of the worship in the sanctuary (as well as in other settings) the lay person can and does excel in creating worship aids and in offering these true gifts of service to the glory of God.

Some of the invocations and offertory words included in chapters 3 and 4 were written by a lay member of a church as a sharing of his poetical talents. He was encouraged to write his poems, and these were used in the sanctuary worship, first of all in the special seasons of Advent and Lent. After a period of time they became a regular part of the sharing in worship. The next step taken was to invite him actually to present the invocation and the offertory words. Because he was a member of the choir, it was possible for him to give leadership from his accustomed place.

Fabric graphics, often thought of as banners, can play an important part in setting a mood, focusing attention, and communicating a message or theme. A person with artistic and sewing talents "got turned on" to banners and offered to make one for Pentecost. She was encouraged to fulfill that offer and proceeded to make a banner three feet by nine feet in brilliant red. On one side she made a burning flame with various textures and colors of fabrics; on the other side she made a three-dimensional white dove descending from the top of the banner with the words "Come Holy Spirit" in bright yellow, readable letters. As a matching pulpit drape she made the symbol of the dove on a flame in the same red fabric. Thus, for the period of Lent, with the large banner showing its two-sided message combined with the pulpit drape in a central setting, the reminder of Pentecost was always present. This also served as a starting place and a reference for the symbols. They became sources for messages. This was so effective that a whole series of such banner and pulpit drapes emerged and was expanded to include matching preaching scarves for the worship leader. The main theme of the season was always present.

It is a rare congregation that does not have one or two people, at least, who are deeply involved in photography. These persons are discerning the beauties of the world around them and are usually ecstatic when invited to contribute their talents to the worshiping community. The pictures themselves, without text or explanation, can convey beauty, order, symmetry, exhaustion, poverty, pity, tenderness, and emotions. Pictures mated with text or titles evoke all manner of affirmations or provocations.

Invite your friends to discover with you new ways of worshiping through the visual arts.

Music is an important part of worship. The music, hymns, anthems, and solos are messages in themselves and must be chosen to blend with the spoken message. It is not enough to say, "I just love this hymn; let's sing it." If worship is to carry a message or a feeling, the music ought to reinforce that and ought not to take off on a tangent. The choir and the soloists are, therefore, an integral part of the sanctuary worship. In some instances music takes up as much of the worship time as the spoken word by the leader of worship. The choir and all the musicians become leaders of worship and should approach their involvement as seriously as does the priest or minister. For the lay person this can be one of the most important leadership roles any lay person can play. Although the singer or musician is the conveyer of the message, the central leader needs to be assured that what is being done musically is a part of the whole. Careful consultation is needed to insure that the best possible match of music and message is achieved. Organists, choir directors, and soloists need to feel the importance of understanding their role in the worship service. It is a partnership. In many ways the worship leader is a lay person to the musician, and the musician is a lay person to the worship leader. When they work together with their various talents and knowledge, worship truly comes alive. Each must respect the other's talents and allow for sharing and mutual respect. When that happens, all become leaders of worship.

Above all, we must remember that one of the continuing needs of congregations is for its leaders to provide insights and leadership for all persons so they may grow in their appreciation of the strength inherent in worship.

RESOURCES

Banners

Anderson, Robert W., and Caemera, R., *Banners, Banners, Banners.* Chicago: Christian Art Associates, 1967.

Ferguson, George, *Signs and Symbols in Christian Art.* New York: Oxford University Press, Inc., 1959.

Ireland, Marion P., *Textile Art in the Church: Vestments, Paraments & Hangings in Contemporary Worship, Art & Architecture.* Nashville: Abingdon Press, 1971.

Laliberte, Norman, and Mellhany, Sterling, *Banners and Hangings: Design & Construction.* Cincinnati: Van Nostrand Reinhold Co., 1966.

Post, W. Ellwood, *Saints, Signs and Symbols.* Wilton, Conn.: Morehouse-Barlow Co., 1974.

Wallace, Gwynneth, ed., *Banners Now.* Montreal: Mount Royal United Church, n.d.

——————, *Banners and How.* Montreal: Mount Royal United Church, n.d.

Weidmann, Carl F., ed., compiled by Loice Gouker, *Dictionary of Church Terms and Symbols*. Norwalk, Conn.: The C. R. Gibson Company, 1974.

Whittemore, Carroll E., ed., *Symbols of the Church*. Nashville: Abingdon Press, 1974.

Wolfe, Betty, *The Banner Book*. Wilton, Conn.: Morehouse-Barlow Co., 1974.

Other Resources

Chapman, Rex, *A Kind of Praying*. Norwich: Fletcher and Sons, Ltd., 1970.

Christensen, James L., *Contemporary Worship Services*. Old Tappan, N.J.: Fleming H. Revell Company, 1971.

_____, *Creative Ways to Worship*. Old Tappan, N.J.: Fleming H. Revell Company, 1974.

_____, *New Ways to Worship: More Contemporary Worship Services*. Old Tappan, N.J.: Fleming H. Revell Company, 1973.

Doerffler, Alfred, *Open the Meeting with Prayer*. St. Louis: Concordia Publishing House, 1955.

Jasper, Ronald C., and Winstone, H., ed., *Prayers We Have in Common*. Philadelphia: Fortress Press, 1975.

Micklem, Caryl, ed., *Contemporary Prayers for Public Worship*. Grand Rapids: William B. Eerdmans Publishing Company, 1967.

_____, ed., *More Contemporary Prayers*. Grand Rapids: William B. Eerdmans Publishing Company, 1970.

Quoist, Michel, *Prayers*. Mission, Kan.: Sheed Andrews & McMeel, 1974.

INDEX

Acts 2:1-4, 18
Acts 3:1-10, 21
Acts 11:19-26, 23
All Together in One Place, 18
At a Time of Change, 68
At Day's End, 41
At the Beginning of the Day, 67

Baptism, The, 58
Be Still, 18
Be Strong in the Lord, 15
Brother Lawrence, 44
Bumper Stickers That Say More, 82

Call to Worship and Offertory Words
    for Advent, 49
Camp Fire, The, 73
Cleansing the Temple, 62
Communion Prayers, 34
Covenant Renewed, The, 64
Crucifixion, The, 65

Dali, Salvador, 85f.
Declaration of God's Goodness
    (Psalm 100), 30
Dürer, Albrecht, 85f.

Easter Morning, 61
Ecclesiastes 3:1-8, 79
Ephesians 6:10-20, 15
Exodus 12:21-28, 64

Family Prayers, 69
First Corinthians 1:17-25, 88
For Families, 68
For the Bread, 34
For the Cup, 35
For the Gifts of Life, 68

General Meditations for Small
    Group Meetings, 14f.
Genesis 1:1-3, 53
Genesis 1:1-12, 82
Genesis 22:1-18, 65
Good News at Christmas, 51

Habakkuk 3:17-19, 31
Hear the Word of the Lord, 21

Hebrews 3:17-19, 22
Hebrews 12:18-25, 60
His Face Is Set Toward Jerusalem, 57

In Autumn, 40
"In Him Was Life . . . ," 16
In Spring, 40
In Summer, 40
In the Beginning, 82
In Times of Loss, 68
In Winter, 40
Invocations, 32
Invocations and Offertory Words for
    Lent, 57f.
Isaiah 2:4, 52
Isaiah 5:1-7, 63
Isaiah 6:1-10, 79
Isaiah 9:2-7, 53
Isaiah 40:1-5, 54
Isaiah 42:1-4, 51
Isaiah 55, 80
Isaiah 55:6-7, 32

Jeremiah 2:4, 13, 21
Jeremiah 7:1-15, 62
Jeremiah 22:1-9, 63
John 1:1-5, 16, 54
John 1:6-8, 54
John 1:9-10, 54
John 4:7-26, 20
John 4:23-24, 20, 32
John 6:32-40, 82
John 8, 84
John 8:21, 83
John 14:1, 84
John 15:16-17, 85
Judges 6-7, 16

Life in Christ, 14
Light of Christmas, The, 52
Litany of the Cross, A, 61
Long View, The, 23
Loving Fellowship, A, 19
Luke 1:5-55, 56
Luke 1:68-80, 52
Luke 2:1-20, 51
Luke 2:29-32, 51
Luke 4:18, 59

Luke 17:11-19, 42
Luke 19:41-48, 62
Luke 20:9-20, 63
Luke 21:1-19, 63
Luke 22:1-23, 64
Luke 22:63–23:49, 65
Luke 24:44-49, 17

"Make My Name," 23
Mark 1:2-8, 55
Mark 10:17-22, 24
Matthew 5:14-16, 44
Matthew 7:7-8, 30
Matthew 13:44-52, 81
Matthew 23:8-12, 58
Matthew 25:35, 83
Meditations and Prayers Dealing
    with Social Concerns, 24
Meditations for Advent, 50f.
Meditations for Board and
    Committee Meetings, 21
Meditations for Church Business
    Meetings, 18
Meditations for Holy Week, 62
Meditations for Youth Meetings, 22
Miracles, The, 59

New Year's Litany, A, 74
No Silver or Gold, 21

Offertory Prayers and Words, 33
Our Stake in the Church, 80
Outdoor, Camping Worship, 72

Palm Sunday Prayer, 61
Peace at Christmas, 52
People Are Too Many, The, 16
Philippians 1:1-11, 19
Philippians 2:5-11, 31
Prayers (In Unison), 29
Prayer for a New Day, 41
Prayer for Illumination, 44
Prayer for the New Year (In Unison),
    30
Prayer for Seniors' Sunday, 38
Prayer of Confession, 37
Prayer of John Baillie, 46
Prayer of St. Patrick, 45
Prayer of Thanksgiving, 37
Prayers of Approach, 36
Prayers of Intercession, 37
Prayers of Supplication (In Unison),
    29
Prayers of the People, 35

Prayers While Visiting, 71
Private Prayers, 67
Proverbs 2:1-5, 22
Psalm 8:1-9, 14
Psalm 19, 82
Psalm 19:1, 72, 73
Psalm 23, 44
Psalm 40:1-8, 18
Psalm 46:10, 18
Psalm 92:1-2, 31
Psalm 95:6-7, 31
Psalm 100, 30
Psalm 100:3, 31
Psalm 124:8, 31

Quietness, 73
Quotes That Provoke, 78

Romans 8:26-28, 23

Schweitzer, Albert, 42
Seasonal Prayers, 39
Second Corinthians 4:7-16, 14
Sentences for the Opening of
    Worship, 30f.
Service for Advent, A, 53f.
Sickness, 72
Sorrow, 71
Stars and the Heavens, The, 73
Stone Rejected, The, 63

Table Graces, 70
Taylor, John W., 46
Teachings, The, 59
Temple Replaced, The, 63
Thoughts and Prayers of Great
    Christians, 41f.
Thoughts for Good Living, 81
"Time is too slow. . . ," 79
Triumphal Entry, The, 60
True Greatness, 58
True Wisdom, 22
True Worship of God, 20

Visitation on Behalf of the Church, 72

Waves of the Lake, The, 74
Weiss, S., 43
Wesley, John, 43
Where Can I Find Eternal Life?, 24
Wonder, 14
Worship Through Paintings, 85f.

"You Are Witnesses," 17